Traces of Hope

Surviving Grief and Loss

Mona Villarrubia

s‡p

St. Johann Press
Haworth, NJ

ST. JOHANN PRESS

Published in the United States of America
by St. Johann Press
P.O. Box 241
Haworth, NJ 07641
www.stjohannpress.com

The paper used in this publication meets the minimum requirements of
the American National Standard for Information Sciences—Permanence
of Paper for Printed Library Materials, ANSI/NISO Z39/48-1992

Composition and interior design by Susan Ramundo
(susan@srdesktopservices.com)

Cover design by G&H Soho Inc., Elmwood Park, NJ
(ghsoho.com)

ISBN 978-1-937943-27-1

Manufactured in the United States of America

To Mal, Malcolm, and James

CONTENTS

INTRODUCTION

Grief is messy. It comes with an assortment of feelings: denial, anger, depression, and a whole lot more. These feelings are often portrayed as stages in a linear process of healing. But the experience of grief is not so tidy. The feelings can arrive in a chaotic jumble or one at a time in a process that is different for everybody. And to complicate things more, you don't experience emotions like denial just once and then move on to another, rather grief is a cycle. Every year on the anniversary of the loss of a loved one, or a catastrophic event of another kind, you relive your loss. It becomes less intense—eventually—but even after years, an anniversary might suddenly throw you under the emotional bus. You have feelings so intense you wonder if it will ever get easier.

But it's not just anniversaries. A scene in a movie, the smell of a certain perfume, a young man with blond hair driving a red car, a song on the radio. Simple everyday occurrences have the ability to send you right back into the swirling cyclone of grief. You are overcome with sadness and tears and even denial. And it can last for minutes, days, or months. Those who tell you it is time to move on or get over your loss have no idea about its true nature: it has become part of who you are. You don't ever get over it; you just eventually learn to get along beside it.

I have experienced three profound types of loss in my life: a childhood lost to sexual abuse, a hurricane that stole six months of my life, and the death of a son—three major traumas, three different kinds of loss, each one challenging my faith in different ways. So, this book is not a sterile, intellectual exercise. The questions I raise here come from a deep, sometimes desperate need: the need to reclaim the hope I once relied on, the hope I tried to offer my students as a teacher of theology, the hope that my son wrote of . . . even as he prepared to die.

In some ways this book is a spiritual odyssey, and typically such books might generate speaking engagements, t-shirts, and affirmation cards. They take the reader from the pain of brokenness to a transformative renewal of faith and hope—and maybe the secret to happiness in seven easy steps! My story travels in the other direction: from a faith-based career and a real sense of living my life in God's hands, to the desolation of feeling that God has let go. What comes next is a slow, sometimes angry, sometimes joyous, ultimately tentative path forward.

If you are looking for a story of immediate spiritual transformation, then this book is not for you. If you need to find comfort in the reassurance that God definitely has a plan and everything happens for a reason, this book will not serve you well. I'm telling you this because I don't want to cause any more pain: grief and loss are too difficult already. But if you are grasping for a raft in the midst of overwhelming tragedy and loss, and its ensuing emotional chaos and spiritual doubt; if you are disillusioned with the response you have received from organized religion; if you are not even sure about God, let alone God's plan, then we are on a similar journey, and maybe we can share the road for a while.

TRAUMA, GRIEF, AND LOSS— LOSING "NORMAL"

The experience of grief accompanies any loss, and feelings of loss can be created by any significant emotional event in one's life.

Chaos Theory and Hurricanes

Is there any order in the universe, or is life just a random, chaotic set of events with no distinguishable pattern or plan? And if God is in charge, why doesn't God answer our prayers for safety from natural disasters?

As we stared at the satellite images of Hurricane Katrina, an immense category 5 filling the gulf and heading directly to the Louisiana and Mississippi coastline, as we looked into the demonic "eye" of the storm, we all prayed for our families and friends. We prayed for those who had waited too long to leave, and those who had chosen to stay behind rather than leave beloved pets or critically ill family members or patients. My family prayed especially for my niece Elizabeth, a nurse on duty in New Orleans East. We had all gathered in a hotel in Houston managed by my brother-in-law. He had paid for a room for each family. But that first forty-eight hours, as we slowly arrived in different cars and family groups, we gathered together huddling in front of one TV. Beth was still unaccounted for.

After the storm landed without apparent catastrophe, we breathed sighs of relief. And then levees were breached and a "tsunami" rolled through New Orleans East and Lakeview. Arial views showed rooftops and water. Everywhere water. Hour after hour the TV revealed more and more awful scenes from around the city, and stories of shootings, rapes, looting and chaos surfaced. We prayed for the horrors to end. We prayed for the government to get aid to

the thousands trapped at the Superdome. We prayed, cried, and prayed some more. No one could sleep. We felt helpless, hopeless. We were all drowning in the gruesome and interminable news coverage. But we couldn't pull ourselves away from the TV. We pleaded with God for news of our niece. We bargained, we begged. Take my house Lord, but let Beth be OK.

Did it do any good, all the prayers, all the bargaining and pleading? Beth was rescued and evacuated safely, surviving being shot at as she was transported by motor boat through the streets of New Orleans East. But was her survival the result of our prayers? What about the prayers of other families that weren't answered? Were their prayers less worthy, their lives less honorable? Does God sit somewhere with a moral calculator making assessments and meting out punishments? Jesus would not portray his Abba, God in such a way.

As the hours passed into days and we began to make an assessment of our situation, it seemed impossible to imagine ever being able to return to New Orleans. It felt as if the government and God had conspired to destroy our city and make it impossible to ever go back to the way things were. Well, there was truth there. It would certainly never be the same.

Jobs, salaries, cell phones, clothing, food. So much to figure out. Luckily we had a laptop with us. A lifeline. But with so many people still dependent on dial-up, communication was spotty, and cell phone coverage was even worse. So many towers down. For a couple of days we clung to each other in that hotel and to the opportunity of celebrating simply being alive. There was a false euphoria created simply by all of us being together and all of us being safe. Slowly, slowly we began to develop separate plans. There were relatives in North Louisiana for some to move in with. Our oldest son wanted to return to New Orleans as soon as the city opened up. My husband and I waited to hear about our schools. What would we do with no job, no insurance? Food stamps? I could do that. If I had to, I could do that. I had gone with my mother to collect our food stamps. She had hated it but she did it. My father worked full-time as a self-employed butcher, but he didn't make enough to raise five children. You do what you have to do.

A week passed. Mal, my husband, and I looked for a temporary apartment. Our son had returned to New Orleans, but the city had closed up again. Word came to us of an evening school for New Orleans Jesuit students at the Strake Jesuit School in Houston. Across the parking lot a smaller number of New Orleans Dominican students were being integrated into the St. Agnes student body. Mal was asked if he would commit to a semester at Strake; I was asked to support the Dominican students and their families. We both said, Of course!

Strake families were taking in New Orleans students and teachers, and we were offered accommodation in someone's pool house. It was one room with a double bed, a microwave, a sink, a small fridge and a bathroom. Sort of like an American college dorm room, but we didn't have to share the bathroom, and we had direct access to a pool. We were so grateful to have a place of our own where we wouldn't feel we were under someone's feet. We bought two lamps, some plates and flatware, and a crock pot. We were set! Wait! No table or chairs? No problem! We unloaded the picnic table from the Honda CRV and bought two folding chairs. A veritable mansion. I think they loaned us a small TV, but quite honestly I don't remember.

Trailers were brought onto the Stake campus for the Jesuit New Orleans administration: a faculty room, a computer and copy room, a counselors' office, and an administrators' office. At the opening assembly Fr. Tony McGinn announced that we would all return to New Orleans, that Jesuit would rebuild, and the Banks Street tradition would continue. We all cried—students, parents and teachers, even McGinn. A strong community was forged in those Jesuit trailers. We were like the pioneers circling our wagons, like the homeless people of God facing a long journey back to the Promised Land. And we would do it together. Everybody had a different set of hurdles, but each of us shared a common tragedy and that knitted us together. I celebrated my fiftieth birthday in Houston with my Jesuit trailer community—that was the best birthday party I have ever had.

A new kind of normal was beginning to take shape. Life was moving on. But the unsettling feeling remained that the world was not an orderly world,

that chaos was not only possible but perhaps inevitable. Many people's assumptions about the safety and security of their lives had proved unfounded. We would never take an orderly life for granted again, or so we told ourselves.

Post Katrina . . . The New Normal

In Houston I had two "jobs." My first position was helping support the dozens of Dominican students attending school at St. Agnes, and assisting the counseling department to coordinate outreach to their parents. Both Dominican and Jesuit had committed to paying salaries to all its teachers wherever we were. Two Dominican teachers ended up in Houston; some ended up at schools in Baton Rouge, and many eventually returned to New Orleans and worked at an evening campus there.

My other position was as a volunteer Administrative Assistant to the Jesuit New Orleans counseling department in Trailer B. I helped process and submit the college applications for the seniors, which was no easy task given that we had no computers and operated with no student transcripts for the first few weeks. We did the best we could until someone braved the National Guard and waded into Jesuit New Orleans to retrieve the computer server. Then we got paper copies of the transcripts; they were gold. Our students' academic futures depended on them.

We were all in survival mode. On meeting fellow New Orleaneans the first question was always, *How did you do?* (You didn't have to add—in Katrina). If they got water in their house, the next question was, *How many feet?* Then, *Have you been back yet?* We learned about MRE's (Meals Ready to Eat). Our oldest son survived in New Orleans on MRE's and water from National Guard distributions. Our second son was away at college. We were living hundreds of miles from home, in a pool room, and we considered ourselves very, very lucky. We were lucky because we had lost no family members. Our newly married niece, Beth, lost her house in New Orleans East, as did all her in-laws. Beth also lost all her wedding gifts. But no one lost their lives. And us? Our house was fine with damage only to the roof and fences from fallen tree limbs.

Flood water had not reached the house; it came up on the grass within an inch of flooding the house, but didn't come in. So, although we were away from home, unlike thousands of others we had a home to go back to. Both our sons congratulated their dad in amazement, Wow dad, you mean all that dirt we put down every year really worked. Damn!

Life in Houston began to take on its own routine, and everybody joked about adapting to the "new normal" of being a Katrina survivor. Houston families donated clothes; we began to develop a support structure; we were managing. Then came reevacuation for Hurricane Rita. That was surreal. It's hard to describe the combination of fear and hysteria that we lived in that weekend. I didn't know what hysteria was until I found myself laughing at the notion of another hurricane and another evacuation, as tears ran down my face and my body trembled from head to toe. But we managed. We drove to friends in Baton Rouge only to have the storm follow us. Four extra families in a three bed-roomed house, temperatures in the 90s and no power. A few days later we were headed back to Houston, praying for open gas stations along the way. Just like our cars, we were running on nearly empty.

The loss and destruction that was caused by Katrina continues; so many years later it is not healed. There are areas of new housing and less and less blight, but some neighborhoods are only just getting back basic conveniences such as grocery stores. And a hospital has yet to be built in New Orleans East. The experience of trauma in the life of a city can be compared to the experience of trauma in the life of an individual—there are effects that will last forever. Changing and mellowing perhaps, but never gone entirely.

New Orleans Devastation

So there we were, living in a pool room in Houston, refugees from a drowned city. Before we began our new jobs our only daily contact was with Frances the dog, our host family's pet, and Harriet ate her own poop. That about summed up my life in September, 2005. Our hosts very kindly installed a telephone line so we could use the computer, and it was to the computer that I turned for something constructive to do.

Writing is how I process, and there was a lot to process. With my background in theology and my years of therapy, perhaps I had some insights into our situation that were worth sharing. At the very least, writing would help me hold my head together.

In early December when officials in New Orleans announced that they would open the city temporarily for refugees to return and check on their homes, we jumped at the chance. We could pick up some clothes and other belongings and check on Malcolm, who was living in the house and earning money gutting houses while waiting for the University of New Orleans to reopen.

What greeted us when we arrived was a city still without power and without services—no police, hospitals, or mail. There was little to no food on the shelves of shops, no restaurants open, no working gas pumps in many places, and, strangely, no sounds of insects or birds. And this was on the good side of the 17th street canal. On the New Orleans side everything was downed trees, standing water, mud, and devastation. Driving along Veterans highway after sundown, you passed from light to darkness, like descending into a level of hell in Dante's Inferno. Streets on the New Orleans side of the canal were completely unlit. Broken power lines waved in the breeze, but there was no power going through them any more. Occasionally you saw a small skiff or motor boat sitting in a front yard, leaning up against a tree, or decorating the neutral ground in the center of the highway. Whole neighborhoods looked as if they had been bombed.

Even in the neighborhoods that hadn't flooded as a whole, certain streets had. And other streets remained blocked because of downed trees and power lines. In every block of every neighborhood where there were still houses, hundreds gaped open to the elements with the carcasses of trees filling what had once been a bedroom or a den. Many of the salvageable houses were covered in blue tarps. And, as families waited for insurance adjusters to turn up, or prayed for an honest contractor, what had been potentially salvageable turned to mold and rot.

Some ex-military compared post-storm New Orleans to wartime. The presence of tanks and armed military personnel in our neighborhoods, and helicopters overhead, confirmed the validity of that comparison. It was like being in a Hitchcock movie but without the soundtrack, and the credits just wouldn't role. I was terrified of my own city and glad to leave before the curfew, when darkness would descend completely on the postapocalyptic scenery.

Malcolm was enjoying the frontier-like experience. He had cleaned our fridge of its awful Katrina funk—weeks of food left in 90 degree plus heat—but he said that despite multiple attempts at fumigation everything he put in it tasted of the funk. Nonetheless, he was enjoying himself. Working with friends and making some money. Having people over to the house. Sharing "war" stories with everybody he met.

Back in Houston, using the Dominican contact information I had collected, I began to reach out online to people from my school community. Of course I had no way of knowing how many of them had managed to set up an internet connection. And then, even if they had access to a computer and to the internet, would they be ready to read reflections on suffering and loss? Wasn't it enough that they were living it? Yes, more than enough. But I needed to write; it was for me much as anyone else, probably more so.

Much of what follows in this chapter began as reflections that I wrote in Houston for my friends spread around the southern states and beyond.

Trauma and Meaning

Prior to August 29th of 2005 I had been teaching high school theology full-time, raising two sons with my husband of then 26 years, and attending regular therapy sessions for unresolved sexual trauma issues. Life wasn't always easy, but it was better than it had ever been before, and I felt blessed. Mal and I loved our teaching jobs in New Orleans. Our oldest son, Malcolm, had returned home for graduate school. Malcolm was working in the International Studies program at the University of New Orleans, and our relationship with him was better than it had ever been. Our second son, James, was on a full

scholarship at the University of Virginia. We were all doing well; life was good! Then Katrina hit and sucked the comfort right out of our lives.

The experience of tragedy has a way of focusing you. Like sunlight burning through a magnifying glass, tragedy gets your attention fast. Past hurts move to the periphery of one's emotional vision. Not forgotten, but no longer the focus of attention. In Houston it was impossible to work on abuse issues while trying to wrap my mind around the loss of my entire city, my livelihood, my normalcy.

I managed to keep my head together with the help of a Houston psychologist who agreed to take me on and help manage my anxiety. And in my spare time I wrote. Sitting with a laptop propped up on the picnic table from my CRV, listening to reports of eighty percent of New Orleans still under water, I began my reflections on suffering. As I wrote, I came to understand how trauma of any kind involves the same basic elements. Suffering is suffering. In the end it doesn't matter whether it is caused by Mother Nature or your own mother, a levee break or the breaking of a vow. The feelings of denial, pain, loss, anger, grief, depression, and isolation and all the rest will be there; the difference will be in the cause and intensity of those feelings. It is common for the experience of trauma to challenge our views on the ultimate issues: the meaning of life, the purpose of suffering, and the nature and existence of God. And those were the topics I wanted to pursue in my reflections.

The Need to Grieve

When we experience loss there is a need to grieve. And loss can be any significant change in one's life—anything from a friend moving away, a change in employment, divorce, a diagnosis of cancer, or the loss of a parent. Trauma involves a particularly intense experience of loss, whether it is sexual assault and the loss of physical and emotional safety and peace of mind, or the destruction of one's city and the loss of one's way of life. Recovering from trauma will require a grieving process. The degree of grieving varies according to the degree of loss that is felt, and the loss varies with each individual—even in shared circumstances. A factor that affects the degree of felt loss is personal history: the current experience of trauma and its subsequent grief and loss will be compounded when there is a history of trauma in a person's life.

The above paragraph bears a reread because it sums up so much of what I have learned about grief and loss. "Felt loss," for example. What does that mean? It means that depending on who we are and where we are in our lives, and what connection we personally have to what is lost, we will feel the loss in a different way. For example, everybody in a family experiences the loss of a family member differently, with differing degrees of pain, sorrow, guilt, and anger. They share the occasion of loss but not necessarily the degree or depth of the felt loss. The loss will be more complex if there is unresolved anger, for example, because that is likely to create guilt not felt by family members who were on good terms with the deceased. Another common example: your divorce might feel liberating to you and yet your daughter may feel a loss comparable to the death of her dad.

As to previous losses compounding the situation, if you suffer symptoms of Post-Traumatic Stress Disorder from a previous trauma, then your symptoms can be triggered by a new trauma or loss of any kind. Simply the imminent threat of Hurricane Katrina could have been enough for you to start experiencing panic attacks. It's as if "normal" anxiety isn't possible. Your level of anxiety can go straight to "extreme," as previous anxieties seem to flow into the new experience despite their completely different origins. This was the case for me. I was already having panic attacks curled up in my locker when Katrina reached a category four.

The Unnatural Experience of Natural Disaster

Unless you have experienced a tornado sweeping through your neighborhood, or a hurricane sending flood waters through your city, or a fire devouring whole swathes of your town and landscape, you cannot understand the kinds of losses these natural disasters involve. The losses range from missing roof tiles to the total annihilation of homes, from temporary separation from friends

and family to potentially permanent relocation in a different state, from the loss of jobs to the loss of loved ones. Whole neighborhoods lost; cities without infrastructures. The losses are always beyond calculation, regardless of how many assessors are employed to figure it all out.

In New Orleans our school community lost a whole semester of curricula and competitive sports. Our seniors lost the special traditions associated with their passage into senior year. All of us lost something; some of us lost everything.

How does anyone deal with losses like these? There are no simple answers. Watching TV footage of natural disasters, people often ask themselves and each other, *What would you grab first?* To the citizens of a natural disaster this is not a rhetorical question. Katrina offered New Orleanians the opportunity to simplify our lives and reorient our priorities. We were reminded that the stuff we accumulate so voraciously just isn't important. We were reminded that family is.

I'm not saying, not for a nanosecond, that Hurricane Katrina, or any disaster like it, can be considered a good thing, but I am saying that good can come from the wreckage. Before good can come from any loss, however, we have to grieve. Sounds obvious, but survivor guilt can make it very difficult to grieve our losses. We might tell ourselves we have no right to grieve because we didn't lose enough. That is like saying, *I have no right to grieve the death of my son because I have another son.* Some parents aren't that lucky. Obviously, this makes no sense. Loss is loss. Every loss needs to be grieved.

Minimizing a loss and trying to stuff feelings will only create problems. If you have suffered a loss, it is important to your health and sanity that you allow yourself the time you need to howl and cry and then just to be sad for as long as you need to. If we do not give ourselves permission to grieve, we will feel separated from our feelings and become hopeless. After a loss, anger is important, tears are important. Finding someone to share them with is important, too. That is why the Red Cross dispatches specialized disaster mental health workers along with food and medical supplies.

In Houston we had a parents' support group at St. Agnes for the parents of the Dominican High School refugees. We just listened to each other, collected emails, stayed in touch, helped with clothing for the students, shared stories, and listened some more. I think many parents were still in shock, and speaking their reality out loud over and over helped it to sink in and helped them to take the next step.

Is My Loss as Bad as Yours?

It's important not to compare losses. Our pain is not unimportant simply because someone else's is bigger or deeper. Someone who loses a pet can be just as devastated as someone who loses a husband, especially if their pet is, to all intents and purposes, their "significant other." And losing precious family heirlooms and mementos in a flood, tornado, or raging fire—things that can never be recovered or reproduced—hurts too. And the hurt is real. We should never dismiss our pain.

In group therapy I have often heard sexual abuse victims deny the significance of their abuse, minimize their struggles, even laugh away their suicidal thoughts, because they didn't believe it was bad enough to be of any consequence. Can we all just give ourselves a break? Loss is painful; suffering is real. Do doctors treating cancer compare the size of tumors and allot increments of compassion to their patients in direct proportion? Of course not!

Another important point: witnessing violence can be as traumatic as experiencing violence; an attempted act of assault on us can be as traumatizing as a completed act. And of course, two millimeters of cancer can be as devastating as two square inches. Whatever the size of the tumor or the severity of the assault, you have lost your sense of safety, your peace of mind, and your sense of wholeness and health, and you are facing the possibility of long term, painful recovery. You are also having to confront your mortality, perhaps for the first time.

So if you are hurting because of a loss of any kind, and of any magnitude, give yourself the compassion you deserve, without judgment, without measurement, without question and without a time-limit.

Letting Go of the Illusion of Control

After Katrina I heard this comment from a Lakeview resident who had lost everything, *It wasn't personal. I just have to deal with it.* What she was commenting on was the fact that God didn't chose to hurt her by destroying her house. It just happened. For many of us that seems insufficient as an answer. Weren't we always told that God was in charge? And isn't what happened all part of God's plan? Doesn't that make it intensely personal? And surely if she had been faithful to God and obeyed the church rules, God would have answered her prayers and kept her and her house safe, right? Apparently not! God doesn't look at prayer that way, it seems.

I am reminded of that joke about the man who wouldn't leave his house during a flood because he believed God would save him. As the water rose in the street, a neighbor offered him a ride out in his truck.

No. God is going to save me, Was his response.

As the water entered his house his cousin came by in a boat and was met with the same refusal. Finally, as the water lapped at his roof, a Red Cross helicopter flew overhead and offered to pull him to safety. Again he refused. And soon he drowned. When he arrived at the Pearly Gates he was really ticked off and demanded an audience with the Almighty.

You promised to save me! He challenged.

God raised his hands in frustration and replied,

But I sent you a truck, a boat, and a helicopter!

I have always sympathized with the man in this joke. He exhibits the kind of naïve faith in prayer that my mother raised me on. Pray for a miracle and God will send back the floods. But I have discovered that prayer doesn't work like that. I have had to let go of my childish understanding of God and my unrealistic expectations for prayer. This too is a form of loss. I have come to accept that I cannot control what happens to me, however much I pray, I can only control how I react to what happens. I cannot control other people's behavior, or protect my sons from heartache and disappointment. I cannot control the weather, I cannot control who gets sick and dies, and I cannot control God.

Letting go of the illusion of control is a necessary step in healing from loss, but that doesn't make it easy.

Characteristics of Grief and Loss

When you are in the immediate throes of a disaster, you don't have the emotional energy to engage in reflection. Who has the luxury of processing an experience of loss when you are living on people's floors, in tents, or in your car? In New Orleans the normal packing for hurrications is three days worth of clothes. We pack because we have advance warning and can choose to leave. But people in New Orleans East who decided to ride out the storm had no time to pack. Breathing a sigh of relief that the hurricane had passed, they suddenly saw a powerful wave of debris-filled water rushing down their streets. It swept their cars away, forcing them into attics, onto roofs, into boats, even into trees. Modern technology has provided us with advance warning for many disasters; but for some situations, like the levee breaches in New Orleans East, and typhoon Haiyan in the Philippine islands, there was simply nowhere else to go.

Eventually, a process of reflection will probably take place, and then a knowledge of the stages of grief and loss developed by Elisabeth Kübler-Ross can be helpful. Kübler-Ross was herself uncomfortable with the popular view that these stages were set in stone. So I will identify them as characteristics rather than stages, acknowledging that they can be experienced in different and repetitive sequence or not at all. This knowledge doesn't make loss easier or healing faster, but it can help us understand where we are, and, perhaps more importantly, where others are in their grieving and why we might feel out of sync.

Characteristics of Grieving[1]

1. Denial

In therapy circles you will often hear that Cleopatra was not the only queen of "de-Nile." Another saying is: If one person calls you a horse that person must be crazy; if five people call you a horse, saddle up! Denial is a natural reaction to a painful reality. Who wants to feel pain? It is preferable to simply deny reality. Denial is usually obvious to everyone except the one in denial, naturally, and it is difficult for the rest of us to accept that we cannot make someone see things as we think they should.

The father of a friend of mine was determined to return to his house in Vinton, Louisiana, after Hurricane Rita (the one that followed right after Katrina) even though there was no power in the area, no water, and no sewage services. He didn't want to accept the truth, so he vehemently denied it, insisting on being brought home. Nothing my friend said could change his mind. After being driven to Vinton and facing the undeniable reality of the destruction of his house and the devastation of his neighborhood, he returned to Baton Rouge stooped and sad, looking all of his 84 years for the first time since I had met him. Denial was no longer an option, and he moved straight to depression.

Denial is a natural reaction to tragedy and can be life saving: it provides us with temporary strength. But "in denial" is not a useful place to stay. The problem with denial is that it disables us from moving on. We remain stuck, using our energy to maintain our denial rather than to grieve and heal. Nonetheless, everyone has to move forward at their own pace. Moving on cannot be forced.

For some New Orleans residents the immensity and power of Hurricane Katrina and the gravity of the call to evacuate were just too awful to accept. Even though forecasters were all in agreement around the country that New

---

[1] *On Death and Dying*, Elisabeth Kübler-Ross.

Orleans was the likely target, some people just couldn't accept it. It's a category three, it won't grow any stronger. It's to the East; we are on the good side so we won't get the worst of it. (Yes, hurricanes have a good side with respect to how much water is dumped on you.) So people went to bed feeling confident and woke up to see a category five heading directly at them. Those who chose to stay in their houses may have been in de-nial; eventually they found themselves in "de-lake." I know, gallows humor, but jokes like this helped us make it through.

Denial can be a useful survival tool, just like humor, but only for a while. At some point we have to face reality. In order to get to a place of hope we have to first accept the pain of the devastation. Unfortunately, the next experience after denial is not usually acceptance and healing but often anger. To those who experience natural disasters, anger is what keeps you going through battles with city hall and FEMA. Anger is your constant companion; anger is your fuel through sleepless days and nights without power.

2. Anger

Once you stop the denial and start accepting the reality of your loss, you are likely to experience anger. It is important to get angry—angry at fate or at life or even angry at God. Anger is not wrong, anger simply is. It is an emotion, and emotions just happen—chemical and physiological responses to thoughts and experiences. Anger is a potent emotion and will find a way of being expressed whether we like it or not. The thing to do is control how we express it and not let it control us.

One of the most unhelpful things that people are told when they are grieving a loss is, *Just put it behind you and move on.* Or, *Just think about what you have, not what you have lost.* Or, *No point crying over spilt milk.* Actually there is a point, and it is a very important one: if we don't allow ourselves to really feel our anger, fear, and sadness, and express these emotions in nondestructive ways, they can never be put behind us. Instead they will always be controlling us.

Anger is a natural part of the grieving process and is often expressed as blame. We want someone to be held responsible. Even though being angry at God may feel like blasphemy, when it comes to natural disasters, we cannot blame a person we can only blame God. After all, God is supposedly in charge of the "Big Picture," so God must have wanted or at least have allowed all the bad things to happen. Yet how could God be All Powerful and All Loving and allow atrocities to occur, allow hurricanes to wipe out whole communities?

I have only recently managed a quick foray onto the battlefield of anger. I am working with being angry about being abused: angry at my parents, angry at my abusers, and angry at God! But getting to this point has been a challenge. Getting angry at my priest abusers was tantamount to getting angry at God, a double blasphemy in my mind growing up. And there is a thick wall of fear wrapped around anger, too. Fear about what my father, or my abuser, or God would do to a little girl who disobeys. I know all the rational answers as an adult, but it remains a difficult web to unravel, nonetheless.

Getting angry is an important part of the process of healing, but anger towards God? It may feel uncomfortable, but being angry with God puts us in good company: both the biblical Job and the historical Jesus got angry with God. So if we are ticked off with the Almighty, I believe we can trust that God understands. In the musical *The Book of Mormon* there is a song that is both beautifully poetic and rhythmic. It just grabs you. It is sung by the inhabitants of a small Ugandan village who then translate the words and, well, suffice it to say the natives are shooting God "the bird."

> *Hasa Diga Eebowai*
> *When the world is getting you down*
> *There's nobody else to blame*
> *Raise your middle finger to the sky*
> *And curse his rotten name.*[2]

---

[2] *The Book of Mormon*, book, lyrics, and music by Trey Parker, Robert Lopez, and Matt Stone.

They sell t-shirts printed with the words *Hasa Diga Eebowai,* and I must admit I really want one. Not out of disrespect to God but in a gesture of human solidarity in the face of the apparent callousness of the Creator.

3. Depression

A definition of depression that has stuck in my mind for years is "anger turned inside out." The theory of transactional analysis suggests that each adult has within him or her a Parent, Child, and Adult ego state. In a crisis event our internal Parent replays messages we learned from our parents. Perhaps, Toughen up. You're overreacting. It's not that bad. Our Child ego state may respond to these familiar messages by dismissing and denying the reality of our pain. Then the Child may shut down emotionally. It isn't safe to have my feelings. I am wrong to feel angry. So the very understandable feeling of anger in response to a crisis is suppressed and silenced. The Adult ego state, which is how we are responding in the here and now, responds to this denial by stuffing our anger and other feelings, and becoming depressed.

In my own experience, becoming depressed means a renewed struggle with the urge to hurt myself—a very angry urge.

Being angry is exhausting. In situations like a disaster or a family tragedy, anger eventually drains every ounce of your energy. And then there is the moment of collapse. Implosion. Deflation. As if someone has let the air out of your balloon. And depression can set in.

For me depression is like that moment when the last visitor left our house after our son's wake and we were left to clean up and there was nothing left to say and he was just gone. It is that moment of absolute emptiness when you know life will go on and you cannot imagine how.

4. Acceptance

Although Kübler-Ross wrote that acceptance was the end of the process of grieving, a more recent view holds that it is in fact just the beginning. The

work known as "grief work" really only begins once a person accepts the reality of their loss. A popular definition of grief work is represented by the acronym **TEAR:**

To accept the reality of the loss
Experience the pain of loss
Adjust to the new reality without that which has been lost
Reinvest in this new reality[3]

After a loss our lives will never be the same. That doesn't mean life can't be as good or even better, but the adjustment, both practically and emotionally, takes time.

How to Keep Going

Breathing. It shouldn't take practice to breathe, but in fact when we are stressed we tend to take shallower breaths, and the lack of oxygen will make us feel tired more easily. Also, if we are trying to change negative thinking patterns it is vital to provide our brain with the oxygen it needs to create these new neural pathways. Psychology meets neurology!

Journaling. Record the significant events of your life and continue to write every day as a way of giving attention to your feelings. One of my Houston evacuee friends wrote what he called the Book of Texadus, inspired by a 41-hour journey out of Houston for Hurricane Rita—the re-vacuation. His very own Exodus journey. He didn't write it to publish, he didn't write to vent anger, he wrote because it helped him make the seemingly surreal become more real, more tangible. He wanted to be able to remember it later so he wouldn't feel crazy.

---

[3]"Four Tasks of Mourning" as developed by J. William Worden's in his book *Grief Counseling and Grief Therapy.*

Keeping a visual record. After a natural disaster people take photos of their houses or what was once their property for assessors. But it's also useful for their own use. The feelings of unreality that often accompany tragedy make it difficult to process and retain memories of the events. Days and weeks flow together. Taking photographs of our houses and our neighborhoods is important not just for our insurance adjustors but also for our own memories and for our family story-telling.

I did something very ghoulish at my parents' funerals for this reason: I took photographs of them in their open coffins. I knew that later I would not really remember the events, and I needed to be able to recall them, to make the moments real.

Walking. I once adopted a chocolate incentive training plan: walk a block or two, eat a Milky Way. Now I'm diabetic so I can't recommend the chocolate part, but walking—definitely! Walking gets you outside into the air and away from the chaos you are living in at home. Walking helps your body, and therefore you, feel grounded. Literally, you connect to the earth and a sense of rootedness, and feelings of floating and unreality become harder to sustain. Walking feeds the senses with sights and smells and sounds. Walking can connect you to neighbors. Walking stretches tight muscles and can help with sleeping. It's an easy, no gym membership required, prescription for better overall health and wellness.

Networking—telling your story. After any major event, good or bad, the first instinct is to share: with perfect strangers, with the mail person, the grocery clerk, the next person in line for food stamps. "Where were you? How did you make out?" It's a good instinct. Indulge it. But also meet up with others intentionally, and talk about how things are.

Sometimes we tell the same stories over and over. But that's okay. It just means we need to be heard by people who understand. Being listened to helps us feel that our story matters, that we matter.

Sharing your feelings. Following a crisis situation it is natural to continue to experience heightened stress, and as a result we have a higher susceptibility

to colds and viruses as we attempt to get back to a state of "normal" again. By simply listening and sharing we can help each other grieve and help each other stay healthy.

Faith. After Katrina I still had faith. I still prayed in a way that came from my very cells. Every part of me had been made to pray; it was how I had been formed. I now find myself in awe of the faith I had then and lonely for it. Even when I struggled with God, God had been real, tangible. I now mourn my faith like the death of a dear, dear grandparent, one who raised me and taught me everything I knew—all the songs and prayers and poetry and beauty of my Catholic tradition; one who sang me to sleep and prayed me to sleep and rocked me to sleep in the comfort of their love. I didn't have a parent or a grandparent like that. But my faith was all of that to me. As a child I clung to my loving, grandparent God and the faith that it represented. In the winter of 2005 I truly felt held by that faith, by that God.

Prayer. People of faith have more than the sciences to help deal with loss, they have spirituality. Prayer may not save houses from flooding, but prayer has the power to heal. And prayer doesn't have to be complicated. If you want to try prayer, just try a five minute deep-breathing exercise and combine it with a short prayer such as the verse *"The Lord is my Shepherd, I shall not want,"* from Psalm 23, one of my personal favorites. Just repeat the first phrase while breathing in and the second phrase while breathing out. If you're not sure about God and Bible verses, try something along the lines of a self-help affirmation, *"I am safe and secure; I have all I need to survive."*

Meditation. I have come to view prayer and meditation as two separate things. Prayer requires a mindset, an intellectual agreement that there is a conversation going on, and therefore an *"Other."*

I approach Meditation, on the other hand, like floating on the present moment. On the days I feel sure of God, I imagine resting in God's embrace, sure in the knowledge that we are never alone, and that I am totally and absolutely loved. On the days I feel less sure of God, I imagine floating on the tops of trees, looking at the clouds, because nature is always present. I don't have to make a decision to believe in nature.

And when I meditate I practice one of the other survival tools I've already mentioned—breathing. Five minutes of "time out." Not much at all, but it can seem nearly impossible to find. So don't wait to find it—give it to yourself as a gift!

Creating a Safe Place: A Therapeutic Tool

Creating a safe place is a tool I've learned in therapy. For victims of trauma, life doesn't feel safe. Survivors of trauma have to process memories of living in a very unsafe world, of suffering unspeakable loss. So what can we do? It is vital to our survival that we have a safe place to which we can retreat. If the world does not seem to hold out such opportunities for safety, then we can create this safe place within us, a safe haven to which we can retreat when the world is full of chaos and tragedy on the outside. It is in this safe place within that we can find peace and calm, love and support, regardless of what is going on in our lives. It is in this safe place that we can spend time with relatives and friends who have passed on and imagine their loving words and the comfort of a loving embrace. And it is in this safe place that we can imagine God being with us and consoling us. How we do this is completely up to us.

When I meditate I visit my "safe place," and when I prepare to journal on a particularly difficult aspect of my healing, I visit my safe place first. My first safe place was an imaginary place in the upper boughs of a magical oak tree. I would close my eyes and go to my special tree house filled with safe, fun and nurturing things. It did not allow anyone in but me. Sometimes, I imagined leaving the treehouse and going for walks on the beach, and I imagined myself as a child playing with some of the good people I have known, a favorite teacher, a friend. Sometimes I have imagined taking a walk with my son Malcolm.

The wonderful thing about this exercise is that it is completely up to you how you develop it. Whether you approach it as spiritual meditation or simply

as the development of a therapeutic safe place, it is about healing. In the development of your safe place you can experiment with images for God if you choose. You can rename God as Divinity or Absolute Love, something that is a nurturing image for you and one that enables you to pray. In twelve-step programs God is called one's Higher Power. I still believe in Goodness and Meaning as ultimate values, and the word God can represent those to me. I would even say that belief in God in this sense is more important to me now that Catholic ritual is not part of my life.

It's hard to form a bond with a value, so sometimes an image comes in useful. God doesn't have to have a description or title, God can be represented by a color or a sound or something in nature, like Elijah's gentle breath of wind. What is important is finding an image of God that you can relate to, that doesn't carry baggage with it, and that is not based on fear.

Elijah didn't find God in the hurricane but in the gentle breeze. I find solace in that. We don't have to look for God in our "storms," we can look for God in the healing from those storms.

> *"Go out and stand on the mountain,"* the LORD replied. *"I want you to see me when I pass by."*
>
> *All at once, a strong wind shook the mountain and shattered the rocks. But the LORD was not in the wind. Next, there was an earthquake, but the LORD was not in the earthquake. Then there was a fire, but the LORD was not in the fire.*
>
> *Finally, there was a gentle breeze, and when Elijah heard it, he covered his face with his coat.*
>
> I Kings 19:11-13

Spirituality is about forming a relationship with God, and we cannot do that if fear is our motivator. I don't want to invite fear into my safe place; fear is what I am escaping from. So sometimes, like Isaiah, I imagine God as a tender mother who comforts her children (Isaiah 66:13). Then I add a rocking chair, a full-bosomed, grey-haired woman, a soft blanket and fuzzy slippers, and I have my picture of the "Fairly-Good Mother." Not a conventional image for divinity but one that works for me.

What Kind of Person Does Suffering Make Us?

A very special community of storm-survivors formed in Houston. Our weeks were a little skewed with a Sunday through Thursday, 3:30–9 pm, school schedule. But skewed was appropriate for us, our whole lives were skewed. On Fridays, students were free to attend football games and dances. Thursdays became the new TGIF night for faculty and staff, and a routine of karaoke and beer—mostly beer. Routines were important. They created structure in those empty hours after school when we returned to our guest bedrooms or pool houses and the enormity of our situation. One Thursday night as we leafed through the karaoke song binder at our table for the *nth* time, the teacher at my elbow announced, *I'm going to do it!* and downed the rest of his beer. His courage had been growing week after week listening to the fearless locals. One local singer had become our hero, an Asian country music fan who would belt out indecipherable country classics in a strong Asian accent. We were raucous and sincere fans and quite sad if he didn't turn up. There was something of the pioneer about him too; we would have welcomed him into our club of exiles. No one remembers his name but he still brings a smile to our faces whenever we recall him.

Adversity can bring people together and bring out the best. I am thinking of those who risked their own lives in the debris-filled flood waters, commandeering abandoned skiffs in order to rescue people clinging to their rooftops and trying not to get swept away. It is also true that adversity can elicit the worst from us, feeding our deepest fears and prejudices. I am thinking of the police who shot and killed New Orleans citizens crossing a bridge into another Parish. The police were afraid for their lives because the people walking towards them were black and from the inner city, yet none of those citizens were armed.

I experienced only compassion and generosity from others in the Katrina months, from the commiseration of a welfare claims officer in Houston (when I applied for assistance before my salary was assured), to the dogged support of my therapist in New Orleans. Although herself a Lakeview resident whose house and everything in it was now literally in the lake, she put aside the chaos of her life and spent countless hours tracking down her clients through a web of contacts.

When our amazing host family paid to run a phone line to our pool house, we were able to get on the internet and at last communicate with friends and family. My family in England, not having much in the way of extra income, held a family collection and set up a bank transfer of hundreds of dollars to my account. My youngest brother James, a music teacher and a member of the De La Mennais Brothers, organized a fundraiser at his school in Liverpool for my school's music program, raising over a thousand dollars and a violin! Getting permission from his provincial to come to New Orleans for a few days, he was able to present the gifts in person at Dominican and offer me some personal support. My favorite moment was when he joined me in singing and playing guitar for the school mass. After communion he presented the gifts and said a few words and was quite overwhelmed by the clamorous response of 800-plus high school girls. They loved his accent, and his words of support for me raised hundreds of *"aw's."* It didn't hurt that he was cute either!

What kind of person does suffering make of us? In Houston I met real live angels who housed us, fed us, and clothed us. I developed long-term friendships I will always prize. Living in one room for four months under the cloud of Katrina could have destroyed my relationship with my husband, but it didn't. Our marriage became stronger, and I became more emotionally resilient.

Following a tragedy a strange thing can happen: on some level there is relief. I came to believe that the tragedy I was living through was the worst that could possibly happen to me; it could only get better from now on. I didn't think God was somewhere weighing people's suffering and spreading it around evenly, I just felt that the law of averages was on my side. I was still struggling with childhood issues, I still suffered from ongoing anxiety and depression, but I had weathered (excuse the pun) Katrina—surely it was someone else's turn for a while.

Along with this sense of optimism about the future I developed a whole new level of personal confidence: I could do something other than teach. I had skills! Working as an Administrative Assistant at the late-night, trailer park Jesuit campus was fun. It meant working with adults but having daily interaction with students. I began to imagine the possibility of leaving the classroom. Not right away. I would stay at Dominican and finish out the school year at least. It was the winter of 2005; I was a Katrina survivor; I could do anything.

Looking for Answers

When you experience life-altering events, textbook philosophy and Sunday morning theologizing may offer only superficial answers or pious platitudes. But the effects of trauma are anything but superficial. Trauma has the power to grasp you at the very core of your being; it shakes you until you have no breath left, and then it demands an answer from you. After Katrina I decided to write a book about suffering and faith. But first we had to return home and finish the school year.

We returned to New Orleans just in time for Christmas 2005, and in January our two schools re-opened. As department head of Theology it was my job to make sure that our teachers and students had what they needed to complete spring semester courses in theology. But things were difficult. The school had lost its library and all its computers; the department had lost all its resources, and I had lost twenty-five years of articles and books. Thankfully my notes were all in electronic form on a thumb drive. Many students had lost everything in their houses including uniforms, textbooks and notebooks. So it was back to basics for all of us.

It was a strenuous task and in April I handed in my resignation. I would not return the following year. I was burned out by a year of living in

crisis-mode. But it was more than that: I had no emotional resources left. I needed to get back to my own healing, and I couldn't do that as a teacher of theology in a Catholic school. In fact, I was beginning to wonder if I could even remain Catholic. There was a question that connected both of these concerns—healing from childhood abuse, and examining my Catholicism— and that was the question of God. What did I actually believe at this point in my life about the existence and nature of a Supreme Being? After a lifetime of praying the Lord's Prayer, and more than two decades of interpreting my faith through the lens of family, had I lost my guiding metaphor—God seen as my Father/Mother?

THE PROBLEM OF A LOVING GOD

How can God be our loving parent and let us suffer unjustly?

God as Parent

A wonderful thing happened to me when I became a mother, the metaphor of God as a parent became achingly real. And for many years it provided me with my foundational insights into the Abba to whom Jesus prayed.

If God is understood as a loving father or mother certain things logically follow:

- As our parent God does not want us to suffer.
- As our parent God cannot always protect us, and our suffering causes God profound anguish.
- God would rather be the sufferer than watch us suffer for even a minute because that's how a loving parent feels.
- God cries with us; God is reaching out to console and support us.
- We will always be loved by God; we can never lose God's love whatever we do, even if we move away and break off contact or do things God doesn't like.
- And however old we get, we will always be God's son or daughter.

"I'm sorry, but this doesn't help me much, right now" you might respond. *"What about the omnipotence (all powerfulness) and omniscience (all knowingness) of God that I was taught about my whole life? Can't God make it so that we don't have to suffer?"* A very good question. If God is loving, and we are God's

children, and God can do anything, why would God allow innocent children to suffer and die?

The question of how evil can exist in God's world is a question as old as philosophy itself. The traditional formulation goes something like this:

- If God is ALL GOOD AND LOVING then God does not want us to suffer.
- If God is ALL POWERFUL then God has the ability to make a perfect world in which pain and suffering do not exist and people always choose good over evil.
- But yet we are suffering.
- So either God is not ALL GOOD AND LOVING or God is not ALL POWERFUL.

The Problem of Evil is a philosophical conundrum, alright, but it's more than that. It's a faith question that demands an answer. Believing in a God who is like a parent requires us to find a sensible answer to the Problem of Evil. No loving mother would allow a child to suffer needlessly if she could prevent it, so again—why would God?

Why Do We Suffer?

There are many traditional attempts at solving this conundrum of suffering in a world created and maintained by a loving God. These "solutions" are referred to as theodicies and include some of those unhelpful things that people tend to say at funerals and wakes:

- Suffering makes you stronger.
- God is teaching you a lesson.
- God is punishing you for your sins, after all none of us are innocent before God.
- It's all part of God's plan, part of the "Big Picture." Everything happens for a reason; it was simply meant to be.
- Suffering is a mystery that we will never understand in this life because we are not God.

It is true: some suffering is useful. Unhappiness can teach us to deal with the lack of instant gratification and the value of working for things we want. It can also teach us compassion for those who have less than we do. The pain of a flame can teach us to pull our hand out of the fire, both literally and metaphorically. The pain of an injection is an acceptable suffering when one is being protected from infection or illness.

But although we may complain, this type of suffering doesn't usually result in existential anguish. What does bother people deeply is the suffering that seems to serve no purpose: illness, disease, disaster, or the evil perpetrated by one human being on another. And the worst is the suffering of the young and the innocent.

Well-known treatments of the problem of evil include *When Bad Things Happen to Good People*, by Harold Kushner, and *The Problem of Evil*, by C.S. Lewis. A more recent book, *Philosophy for Dummies*, contains a whole chapter on the issue. Given the raison d'être for the "Dummies" series—simplifying complex issues and processes into digestible bites illustrated by catchy icons proclaiming Warnings, Great Ideas, and Tips—meriting a whole chapter shows how important the issue is thought to be. In the bulleted, sound-bite sized, summary of all of Western philosophy, a chapter is massive. And what is the author's conclusion to the problem of evil? Basically, if you think you have an answer you haven't understood the question!

The conclusion of Dummies is the same conclusion offered to Job in the bible. In the biblical story Job has lost all his property, all his children and their spouses, all his livestock, and finally his own health and standing in the community. In the Poem, Chapters 3–42, Job's friends offer suggestions as to why he is suffering: Job must be a sinner, or he must be paying for the sins of his children or ancestors. Job summarily rejects these answers. After much gnashing of teeth and demanding that God answer him, Job finally receives a response. God tells Job that suffering is a mystery, and because Job isn't God, Job cannot expect to understand. Then Job finally says to God, (paraphrase) I quit! I don't think I'll ever get a straight answer from you and it's all just

beyond me. And he resigns himself to his suffering. Not a very good answer, but isn't that how life works out most of the time? We don't get an explanation for the really awful, random, stuff that happens to us, however much we pray for one. Not a particularly satisfactory answer, but as the Dummies author, Tom Morris, points out, *"Any theism that didn't ultimately point to mystery would not be a very believable world view."*

The book of Job actually presents more than a single response to the problem of evil. The "it's a mystery" answer is presented in the main text of the poem, and a completely different one is set out in the prose Prologue and Epilogue. According to the Prologue, Job's suffering was a test of his faith, and, because he remains faithful to God despite all his suffering, the Epilogue tells us he is rewarded with a double portion of all the property he had previously lost, and ten more children to replace the ten dead ones. Lucky wife!

The Epilogue answer, that if I'm good and remain faithful I will get back everything two-fold, obviously doesn't work for disaster victims. God doesn't build people two new houses for every one that is lost. But Job didn't believe in heaven, so God had to give him justice in his lifetime. We have heaven to look forward to, responds the Christian apologist. We don't get the two houses now we get a room in God's great mansion in the afterlife.

The implication of this latter view is that God will make everything right for all of us in heaven. This view may be the Christian response to the book of Job's facile "double of everything" conclusion, but I don't take much comfort in it. Looking forward to a flood-free city in heaven isn't much consolation to those who've lost everything. So the Dummies author, Tom Morris, and the author of the Poem in the Book of Job have it right, in my opinion.

If you are determined to find an answer beyond the "It's a mystery!" response and are looking at the alternatives in the list above, you will soon discover that there is no single answer to the Problem of Evil that works in every situation, and sometimes people's attempts at answers can be quite hurtful. Take, for example, the situation of a mother who has just lost a two-year-old child to cancer and is told by a well-meaning friend, *"Well at least you are young enough to have another child. Maybe God just wanted you to learn something from this to help you be a better parent next time."*

This actually happened to a friend of mine. But can we imagine that our God—Jesus' Abba Father, the Psalmist's Good Shepherd, Isaiah's Mother nursing her child at her breast—would want a child to get cancer because the mother needs to learn to be stronger or a better person? Would God send a hurricane as a punishment for our sins or to teach us the importance of people over possessions? According to some Protestant preachers, this is exactly what God does. I am happy to say that Catholic teaching does not support such a didactic interpretation of suffering. But how do we explain the suffering of innocent children? And what about the hundreds in Katrina who drowned or died of heat exhaustion on crowded interstate overpasses, or had heart attacks because of stress? What lessons was God teaching them? Did they die to test our faith? Obviously it didn't help their faith! In 2013 thousands were killed by Typhoon Haiyan in the Philippines. In some towns there was no one left to learn a lesson. Did they all die to teach the rest of the world some compassion?

Okay, so what if we dispense with faith answers altogether, does the philosophical problem of evil go away? Not really. The problem of the goodness of God goes away if there is no God, but what about the nature of the universe in which we find ourselves? Without belief in God one is still faced with the issue of evil and injustice as a reality of our human experience. The idea of a chaotic, amoral, meaningless universe is not at all comforting. If one at least believes in God, one believes there is an answer, ultimately, even if we don't have a clue as to what it might be.

What Would Jesus Say?

This is a piece from a blog called A Conversation with Jesus the Nazarene, where I have inner dialogues with "Jesus." Not the real Jesus, of course, rather my inner attempt to know Jesus. Totally imaginary conversations, yet sometimes I learn great things from them.

Hurricanes, they're only natural, right?

Hurricane Irene is busy disturbing the residents of our Nation's capital this evening. Northern politicians will no longer be able to sneer that New Orleaneans were crazy to go back to their homes and rebuild after Katrina. Let's see if they consider relocation after Irene. Maybe move the Statue of Liberty to Las Vegas?

But there is a religious issue here, too. I wonder how many Sunday homilies from the ministers of the "righteous" Right will reference God's punishment or God's Plan. People have been using natural disasters as a way of pointing out the sins of others since . . . well since the Bible at least. We all remember the plagues . . . God's punishment on the sins of the Egyptians, and Job's dead children and his boils . . . who can forget those boils. Even though Job swore he wasn't guilty of anything, his friends suggested that maybe it was his arrogance in denying any sins that was his sin. Poor Job couldn't win.

> **(Jesus)** *Do you have a point to make, or is this just a general rant about the Bible? Why are you assuming that people will respond ignorantly and use the hurricane as a way of criticizing the government . . . the sins of ObamaCare bringing down the Wrath of God?*

Okay. I suppose I am assuming the worst. And good job keeping up with our politics, by the way!

I try!

I do actually have a point, though. Isn't it time to let go of the boils and plagues view of God? I mean, we know how climate works; it doesn't require divine intervention to end up with hurricanes in August. They happen every year.

But in Washington?

Come on!! You too? Is this a God Conspiracy Theory from the Son himself?

Just kidding.

There is a bigger problem here than science versus superstition. Regardless of how sophisticated human understanding becomes, the question remains: Why now? Why them? Why me? It is natural to take suffering personally. Suffering is one of the most personal things ever. Perhaps it makes people feel safer if they can explain disasters in terms of punishment: the logic of punishment is more palatable than the idea of random, irrational tragedy. Who wants to live in world of chaos and unpredictability, after all?

You are right, I feel. People do want the comfort of believing that God is in control, like a cosmic Parent.

Well, God is our Parent, right?

Father, Mother, King, Judge. These are all metaphors. Remember your biblical studies. Why is it when faced with fear people immediately forget reason.

Sorry. Sorry. Of course I know that God-Talk is all metaphor. But YOU know the real answers. Does God mess with the weather? You can tell me. I won't tell ANYONE.

Can we focus here? There is a reality that is bigger than what you see or feel. There is a universe that is more immense and complex than your instruments can currently measure. You need to let go of the child-like need for a straightforward, immediate, concrete answer to every question, and a logical explanation for the source of every fear.

The weather is the weather. It will do what weather does. God is God. God will do what God does. These two Truths do not operate on the same level of reality.

Look further. Seek higher Truths. Don't get caught inside your own very imme-diate, limited, paranoid view of suffering and merit.

Now I'm paranoid. Nice!

I'm just trying to break you out of this way of thinking. Didn't mean to sound so critical. But really! Do parents spend every waking second controlling their chil-dren's environment? Okay, maybe some try. But are they successful? No. Their chil-dren will still get hurt, make mistakes, suffer for no apparent reason—the whole human spectrum of experience. Sometimes there just isn't an immediate, personal, specific reason for tragedy. Tragedy just happens.

Wait, are you saying God is our parent? And are you saying that God cannot control events like the weather?

I'm using your metaphor, which by the way is quite useful, but no, I'm saying that when it comes to natural disaster Why? is the wrong question.

And the right question is . . . ? Come on, a little help here.

Good News, or Not so Good?
Did Jesus provide an answer?

When searching the Bible for answers to the problem of evil and suffering, the first point of reference for Christians should be Jesus, not Job. Jesus was Jewish, and the Old Testament contains the scriptures he studied and prayed. And what was the nature of the God Jesus that believed in? Was it the vengeful angry God of much of the Old Testament, or the compassionate God found in some passages of the prophets and psalms? In the images Jesus chose to use for God, it is clearly the latter.

Despite what some Christian ministers were preaching after Katrina, it doesn't make sense to view Katrina as a punishment for homosexuality, pro-miscuity or gambling. If it was, God's aim was way off, as I've suggested. And quite honestly such a God is only attractive if those being hammered are our enemies and God is doing what we consciously or unconsciously want to do ourselves but can't without social repercussions. To those who basked in righteous indignation before TV screens showing scenes of horror and carnage in New Orleans, I ask, *How can you worship the kind of God you believe in? Don't you worry about your own imperfections and wonder about your own reckoning?* Personally, I can't believe in a "hit man" God. And what is more, I don't think Jesus believed in such a God.

Jesus and the Problem of Evil

There are two significant aspects of Jesus life and teaching that deal with suffering and the Problem of Evil:

First, Jesus modeled how to respond to the suffering of others and our own suffering: with compassion, grace, and faith, even when things make no sense and we are wracked with doubt— as he was on the cross.

Second, Jesus portrayed God as Abba—a "dad" foolishly (in the eyes of society) besotted with his children. A dad who wants nothing more than to have his children home safe.

Let's unwrap these a little more.

First: Jesus' response to suffering

Jesus taught that physical sickness was not the result of sin. The man born blind (The Gospel of John, Chapter 9:1-3) was not blind because of his own sin, obviously, but neither was he blind because of the sin of his ancestors, a response Job's friends had suggested to Job as an explanation for his terrible suffering. Jesus' actions suggest a view that was the antithesis of the popular Jewish theology of the time. Jesus didn't offer an alternative explanation for sickness, but he healed the suffering he came across. Why would he heal people if he believed God was punishing them in a way they deserved? He was not a theologian; he was a rabbi—a teacher, and his primary methods were parable and Midrash (reflections on passages from the Torah). So what Jesus

offers is a belief about what suffering is not (it's not God's will) and a model for responding to suffering—compassion and healing.

Christians are challenged to follow the example of Jesus and to trust in God even when we are full of anger, fear, and pain. We are challenged to forgive our persecutors, our abusers. This is the most difficult thing Jesus asks of us, but it is the crux of Jesus' teaching, and it is what Christians agree to every time they pray the Lord's Prayer . . . forgive us our sins as we forgive those who have hurt us. But who do we forgive for our sickness, untimely death, or experience of natural disasters? Maybe we are called to forgive God. Let's pause here a moment. Forgive God? That's a major shift for most of us. Does God need or deserve our forgiveness? Maybe God couldn't do anything about it after all. Maybe God is not all-powerful? (More on that in the next section, What Kind of World?)

Second: Jesus' teaching about the forgiveness of God: The "Foolish Father"

In the Parable of the Prodigal Son, have you ever noticed how gullible the father seems to be? He lets his son take his inheritance and fritter it away. And every night the father walks out to the crossroads hoping and praying to see his son coming home. When his son does return home at last—poor, hungry, and asking for help—the father doesn't punish him. He doesn't even say, *I told you so! I knew you wouldn't make it on your own.* What does this foolish, doting father do? Certainly not what was considered "just" according to Jewish law, or even fair according to traditional parenting rules: he ignores his "good" son and throws his wayward, selfish son a party for which he spares no expense. His love for the wayward son is greater than any wrong this son has committed, and the good son is rightly miffed! I mean, where is the justice in that?

The father in the Prodigal Son story is how Jesus' understands God: waiting patiently, never giving up hope, already forgiving us. What a wonderful, foolish love. Imagine how this man's neighbors in the story would have ridiculed him and how the teachers of the law would have disdained him.

How does this speak to those of us who have suffered tragedy and loss? If we apply the teaching presented in the Parable of the Prodigal Son, and previously noted in the healing of the blind man, we can reasonably surmise that none of our suffering was intended by God; rather God desires us to be healed and will wait for us forever if we have turned away. Pointless death and destruction, painful vengeance and suffering, are not the *modus operandi* of the God that Jesus prayed to.

Where does that leave us? Who's in Charge? Who's to blame? It is clear that Jesus' Abba/Father God would not have a Big Plan that included children dying of cancer, hundreds drowning in floods, or losing their homes, jobs, businesses and communities, or thousands dying in earthquakes and tsunamis. Jesus doesn't tell us why we suffer, but he shows us the kind of person we can choose to be in response to suffering, and the kind of God who is with us in our suffering. It may not be the answer we were looking for, but it's what Jesus offers.

Perhaps, then, to refer back to, *What would Jesus say*— the question to ask is not *Why do terrible things happen*, but *How are we called to respond?*

But couldn't a perfect God create a perfect world or at least one in which only the evil suffer, a world without the holocaust, without ethnic cleansings? And if God isn't directly responsible for natural disasters and disease, is life just a random, chaotic set of events with no distinguishable pattern or plan, one that God merely watches unfold?

Maybe God Doesn't Believe in Justice

News Headlines

- ~ An innocent man is executed.
- ~ A murderer gets off on a technicality.
- ~ Thousands of men and women are blown up in a high rise office building as they start their day.
- ~ Male and female military personnel are shot to death in foreign countries by the civilians whose freedom they are fighting for.

- Wealthy politicians further corruption and cronyism while significant healthcare legislation is ignored.
- A pedestrian is killed on a sidewalk by a twice-convicted drunk driver who walks away without a scratch.
- A hurricane kills over a thousand of Louisiana's poorest and most powerless.
- A typhoon devastates the Philippines.

It is easy to become angry at God when you read these kinds of headlines. How could God let this happen? Our world is imperfect, okay, but shouldn't there be evidence of fairness? If the world was created by a just and loving God, shouldn't there be evidence of that justice and love? It makes me wonder, maybe God isn't just. Job wondered the same thing. So did C.S. Lewis after the death of his wife. Lewis even went so far as to speculate that God might be evil, a Cosmic Sadist. Neither of these men denied the existence of God, just God's goodness. For me it makes more sense to deny God's existence: no God means no divine plan and no expectation of justice. But I don't sit comfortably with atheism.

A closer examination of the news headlines reveals not divine but human injustice and evil. Even the reference to Hurricane Katrina reveals human wrongdoing. For one thing there is the existence of profound poverty in the wealthiest country in the world. And then there's the political corruption that allowed a levee system to be built, and supposedly inspected yearly, without its fundamental unsoundness ever being discovered or at least revealed to the public.

Did God send Katrina as a punishment on the sins of New Orleans? Apparently not, because Bourbon Street in the French Quarter, the center of "sin city" as the world often portrays New Orleans, didn't even flood and was one of the first neighborhoods to be up and running. Maybe God has bad aim and miscalculated the trajectory of the storm? Maybe God didn't foresee the breaking of the levees? Obviously these arguments make no sense in a theistic world view.

What Katrina revealed to the world was not the nature of God's justice but the nature of human corruption. Inspection of the levee system post-Katrina revealed that the levees were built on foundations that went down only two thirds of the required depth. Someone cut time and materials and, as a result, over a thousand people died. In the end it wasn't the storm that did the most damage; it was human corruption. It wasn't God who deserved all of our anger for Katrina after all. Yet, the death of innocent people from drowning or dehydration or heat exhaustion, is still difficult to reconcile with God's love. The debate about whether the storm or human corruption was ultimately responsible is little consolation for the families of the victims.

The Best of all Possible Worlds?

According to the optimistic philosophy of Gottfried Leibniz, our world is as good as it can possibly be. Any other world God could have created would have ended up with even more evil and suffering in it than this one. You may have read Voltaire's novel *Candide* and come across this phrase, "the best of all possible worlds." But *Candide* is actually a satire suggesting that such an optimistic view of the world is unwarranted.

What happens when we apply Leibnitz's view to our experience?

What Kind of World?

The photographs of Hurricane Katrina were awe-inspiring! That giant, swirling mass filling the Gulf of Mexico! If Katrina was indicative of the power of God, then I understand the fear and trembling of the Old Testament prophets. Awesome, terrifying and so tragically destructive. If Katrina wasn't the work of God directly, it certainly happened in God's world, and we are still left with the question, *Why?* Not, *Why does suffering happen in general?* But more narrowly, *Why does the natural world contain such destructive power? Why can't nature be perfect even if humans can't be?* Catholic theologian John Haught has an answer that makes sense to me. I will paraphrase it here.

If God had created the world to be perfect, then the world would have been part of God who is Absolute Perfection. But then God would have been alone, because there can only be one Absolute Perfection. And God, whose very nature is Love, wanted there to be someone to love. So God had to create a world that was separate and distinct from God's nature and God's perfection.

In order for God to eventually be known and loved by an intelligent, self-aware being, the natural world and all its life forms had to grow and change and develop as separate and distinct from God. In order for there to be a Lover and a Beloved, both the I and the THOU that constitute our relationship with God, there had to be both Perfection (God) and Imperfection (not God).

Philosophically, I find this very appealing. According to Aquinas' famous arguments for the existence of God, there can only be one First, Unmoved Mover, one Uncaused Cause, one Absolute Perfection. That makes logical, good sense. It doesn't address the question of how Absolute Perfection came to be or why, but it makes it clear that there is an ontological difference between human nature, human "being," and God's Being.

One thing we can be sure of is that we do exist. If you're not completely sure, I refer you to Rene Descartes, who made a convincing argument in the 17th century for the reality of existence (apparently it was in question at the time). Despite his best attempts, however, he couldn't successfully segue his argument for human existence into a convincing argument for God's existence (according to other philosophers such as Leibniz), which had been his original goal. Nonetheless, he was right about us—we are here, we exist, and we can ask, *Why? Why would a Perfect Being, if such a Being exists, want or need to have a relationship with anything?*

Like the proponents of Process Theology, John Haught understands God not as a static Being but as One who is "becoming." Haught rejects the classical view of God as transcendent (beyond human experience) and immutable (unchanging), disputing the assumption that perfection necessitates an unchanging nature. If God loves us, is truly engaged in a relationship with us—and all monotheists believe that is so—then God must continue to change in response to us. We are always changing, and our needs are always changing. And if someone really loves us he or she will have to be flexible, willing to bend, open to change. Anyone in a relationship, especially a parent, knows this truth. We are told that God loves us, that love defines God. If so, God must logically be open to change in response to loving us, and in response to being loved by us.

Does a process view of God explain the problem of God's plan and our free will? The process view suggests that every time we exercise our free will, God has to adapt. Every time nature throws us a curve ball, God waits to see how we might be helped. This is a very dynamic view of God. Of course philosophically God is understood to be outside of time, and so to say that God changes doesn't have to mean that God is lacking anything or adding anything at any point; God simply is. But the mode of God existence, God's Godness, God's "isness" if you like, is dynamic not static. Maybe that swirling cloud formation of Katrina was more like God than I realized. Such immense power responding to subtle changes in temperature and pressure, wind direction and air currents.

Our planet is a living organism with all kinds of intertwining forces at play. It is constantly changing, and its patterns of change have nothing to do with good or evil, sin or punishment. Nature behaves as nature behaves; there is nothing personal about natural disasters, diseases, or death. My friend was right about that: nature is not controlled by a moral code. I don't believe, therefore, that God chooses who will get cancer and die in pain, or who will pass gently on in their sleep. I don't believe that God chooses where hurricanes will go based on the sins or prayers of the people in its path. I believe that what matters is not why we are suffering but how we respond to it, and what kind of person we become as a result.

Rabbi Harold Kushner, author of *When Bad Things Happen to Good People*, dealt with the personal tragedy of a child who dies of an incurable condition: progeria, the aging disease. This tragedy caused him to rethink everything he had once felt so secure in believing about suffering, prayer, and God. He writes that prayer doesn't change God, it changes us, a sentiment that echoes the writing of Christian author and novelist C.S. Lewis in *The Problem of Pain*. Although God answers our prayers, the answer may not be what we want to hear, or may not be the miracle we hoped for.

After his son Aaron's diagnosis at age 3, Kushner prayed fervently and constantly for a cure. It didn't materialize. Aaron died at age 14 weighing no more than 25 pounds, in a body ravaged with the signs of old age. Kushner's faith in an all-powerful God was shaken. But after four years of reflection he became aware of an unexpected miracle in his life: his marriage had survived Aaron's death and had become even stronger as a result. It wasn't what he had prayed for, but he was nonetheless grateful for this sign of God's grace.

What have you been praying for, and what miracles have gone unnoticed? Kushner would suggest that if we take the time, we will discover God is at work in our lives in many small and perhaps not so small ways: in the generosity of strangers, the hospitality of friends, the love and support of family, even in the power and magnificence of nature. We may not have all our prayers answered, but, according to Kushner, it is possible to discover God is with us in our tragedy and loss.

THE SEARCH FOR MEANING—
FROM NIETZSCHE TO MOTHER TERESA

Unless one sees the possibility of life having meaning,
why bother discussing God or Faith or Suffering?

When Theology Becomes Personal

My issues with God and suffering didn't surface for the first time with Hurricane Katrina. The issue of innocent suffering in a world created by a loving God has been a challenge to my faith since adolescence. It eventually became part of my teaching because I needed answers as much as my students.

I entered teaching in the late '70s excited by the changes brought about by Vatican II. A divinity degree from a Jesuit college had prepared my mind well to teach Catholic history and doctrine. To a great extent theology was an academic exercise for me at this point: I was excited by the subject matter more than I was by my students.

Then in the mid '80s I enrolled part-time in a Masters program at Loyola, New Orleans, and became exposed to World Religions and Feminist Theology. It was then that I realized how narrow my studies had been up until that point. For the first time in my life the patriarchal underpinnings of Catholic doctrine and church structure became glaringly obvious. And whereas at one time a "fatherly" God and Church might have been a consolation, it wasn't any more. If God was not male, God didn't have to be addressed using male metaphors. The Bible even provided feminine options. Who knew! And Mary of Magdala (Magdalene) was not a prostitute; nowhere does the bible refer to her that way.

At first I didn't believe my professor when she shared this information, so she challenged me. I did the research and became quite angry: the reformed prostitute story was a homiletic creation of Pope Gregory the Great in 591. The Mary of Magdala in the New Testament, on the other hand, was portrayed in the Gospels as the first witness of the Resurrection, the first apostle—one "officially sent" with the message of the resurrection and with the authority of Jesus to convey it. Mary of Magdala's true role in Christian history was not news to bible scholars and priests, so why then was the "reformed prostitute" fiction still being preached? Perhaps priests decided that people in the pews were just not ready to hear the truth. The story of a reformed prostitute accepted and loved by Jesus gave such hope to sinners, why take that from them. Or was it that the pivotal role of a woman in the formation of the Church was just an unacceptable truth to the priests themselves?

The Masters program challenged participants to synthesize all that we learned and then apply it to our own faith journey and teaching. If I was to enter into this process, I had to leave the rational and therefore safe level of engagement in theology—separated conveniently from my personal abuse story—and ask myself how my faith made sense in the light of my childhood experience. The transition from academic to personal was an uncomfortable transition.

My discomfort soon became more than a matter of theology—priesthood and liturgy began to feel offensive in different ways. With only men on the altar, where was I, a woman, represented in our liturgy? Why did we have to say, *For us men and our salvation . . .* ? Couldn't our language for humanity, if not for God, easily move into an inclusive form without disturbing our theology? Simply by dropping one pronoun in that statement it becomes inclusive, *For us and for our salvation . . .* And why were so many stories of women in the early church not included in our lectionary—the book containing all the readings for the different yearly cycles?

I struggled with a growing sense of unease with Catholic practice, and hovering on the periphery of my attention were growing numbers of stories about serial pedophiles in the Catholic priesthood. But I wasn't ready to pay attention to that issue just yet. The risks of looking at that were too great.

It is said in theology-teaching circles that sometimes you teach what you need to learn. It was certainly true for me. Soon after completing my Masters, I accepted a position which involved the creation of a new senior theology course. Wanting to practice my graduate school theory, I surveyed my new senior class to discover their issues with religion, faith, and the church. Not surprisingly, some of them were questioning everything religious and were, at best, agnostic. Others were where I had been as a senior—idealistic, committed, and pious. The rest were all points in between.

Something that did surprise me was the philosophical sophistication of my students. At seventeen, questioning my faith had been the farthest thing from my mind. Just as well, really. If I had looked too closely at my faith, it probably would have unraveled, and I would have unraveled along with it. So, instead, I chose to engage in academic study, unconsciously protecting myself. But now, in my late thirties with degrees in theology and religious education to insulate me from losing my faith, it was time to look at some of these questions. Because I was doing my own searching, facing challenges to Catholicism from my seniors didn't intimidate me. I admit. I was a bit of a zealot in some ways. I truly believed that, overall, the traditions and teaching of the Catholic Church were worth defending, even though I personally believed some of them needed to change.

The teachings of Vatican II provided the jumping off point for the course. I wanted my students to understand the excitement we had felt in the '70s, discovering that our Church was ready to embrace the modern world and was open to change. Vatican II revealed a Church not only willing to change but committed to change, and it remained committed until the 1990s, righting its wrongs, including lay people in its understanding of vocation and priesthood, listening to the voices of female theologians, recognizing the Truth of God in other world religions, and including good people of faith from all religious traditions in its understanding of salvation.

Vatican II was good stuff! Exciting. Exhilarating! I truly felt like an apologist for Catholicism, and I was absolutely sincere. It was 1994, and I was on a journey back to my theological roots and toward a renewal of my faith in Catholicism and hoping to take my students with me.

At some point in the future the incongruity between what I taught and the behavior of my Church would become apparent to me. At that point I would face a far more fundamental question: was working for the Church actually a form of trauma bonding in which I was living out an unhealthy and unconscious relationship with my abuser on an institutional level? And once aware of that possibility, could I choose to continue teaching religion without enabling the system that enabled my abusers?

But years would pass before I felt ready to ask those particular questions.

Developing a Course Based on Questions

Over a few semesters the new senior course became focused less on doctrine and history (they weren't as excited about the influence of Platonic dualism as I was!) and more on fundamental questions of philosophy and theology: the Existence of God, the Meaning of Life, the Problem of Evil and Suffering, the Nature of Faith, and the Theology of Grace. The more traditional students appreciated an introduction to classical Catholic theologians; the agnostic students wanted to make sure they could get A's without agreeing with Catholic teaching—no problem. The religiously curious were excited to learn new ideas and experience meditation and mindfulness; they felt very subversive, even though I told them meditation was an ancient Christian practice. I took it as a sign of success when two students asked me to accompany them to worship services at a Buddhist temple and a Unitarian Universalist church. I wasn't glad they were considering giving up being Catholic; neither of them were practicing Catholics anyway. I was glad that they were considering creating room in their lives for spirituality and a faith community and not just giving the tired, I can pray on my own at home response.

So, in general, with some exceptions of course, the class was a success with the seniors. But what would their parents think? On the first parents' night I opened my remarks with some commiseration: As a parent of preadolescent boys I know what it's like to face the Sunday morning challenge regarding church. I don't look forward to the teen years, because my boys are going to be bigger than either of us. Right now I use bribery, usually donuts. That drew a laugh. I was right, though! Malcolm was taller and heavier than either of us by the time he was thirteen. And in his later teens bribery had to turn to blackmail around use of the car. It seemed important enough to make him go to church but would I handle it the same now? Probably not. I think I would invite him to investigate other churches, other faiths, and I would go with him to a weekly service, making that the bottom line not Catholicism. It wasn't really about the rules or the Eucharist. It was about the sacred time of praying as a family. But that is not how I came across, I know.

I told the parents of my seniors that challenging the faith of one's parents was a natural and important stage in faith development. I also shared that, statistically, many young people stopped attending church and didn't return until they were considering marriage or raising children. But that many did return. The good news for the parents was—and there was good news I assured them—young adults are often very spiritual and very interested in pursuing a relationship with God. The Spiritual Autobiographies of my students had confirmed this for me. I encouraged parents to ask their daughters about their ideas about God or Divinity. I am happy to say a few families did embark on some interesting dinner-time conversations, and some parents expressed how they began to share philosophy books and ideas with their daughters for the first time.

The course was a journey, I explained, that would take their daughters on an exploration of theology and philosophy from Nihilism to Grace, from Nietzsche to Mother Teresa. Their daughters would be challenged to think and allowed to question. I recommended ongoing conversations about our course material.

With the exception of one set of parents, who gave me pamphlets on Eucharistic miracles and nervously offered to arrange Catholic guest speakers for the class, (I think they had masses said for my misinformed soul), the overall reaction was positive. And here was the wonderful part: in each group of parents that first night, and every Parent Night thereafter, there were those who expressed their own interest in my course and asked if I would consider offering a course for adults.

Over many semesters the core issue—of the course and of my life—became the need to find meaning in the face of evil and suffering. If there is a God, then life must have meaning, and suffering—innocent suffering anyway—can't be God's will. We examined the writing of C.S. Lewis in response to the sudden death of his wife, Harold Kushner on the loss of his son, Viktor Frankl on the Holocaust. We watched video clips of Akira Kurosawa's *Dreams* dealing with the tragedy of war. We read excerpts from the poetry of Elizabeth Barrett Browning and Gerard Manley Hopkins. Perhaps I had too much material for one course, but somehow it worked.

The life story behind a writer's ideas, and the back story to major events in Catholic history, was always as important to me as the ideas and events themselves. Augustine's theology of Original Sin, for example, is best understood in the context of his personal struggles with self-loathing and guilt. Nietzsche's bitterness and cynicism was fed by an incredible amount of physical and psychological pain in his life. C.S. Lewis' faith struggle was precipitated by the death of his wife. At that moment all he had written about the love of God turned to dust and he wondered if perhaps God was a Cosmic Sadist. I showed my students that the truth of an idea is many layered; and if we can understand what lies behind the idea, the context in which it developed, we are better able to make rational decisions about its merit and about whether it is time to let it go. The same was true about Church history: the Nicene Creed developed in response to heresies; the Council of Trent was a direct response to Luther; Vatican I was a reaction to the Enlightenment.

Teaching my senior course nurtured my mind; teaching my seniors nurtured my faith. My favorite days were the ones when students shared their projects of art, poetry, short stories, and research. They had such insight, such courage, and so many gifts. They taught me so much.

The Search for Meaning—from Nietzsche to Mother Teresa

"The Meaning of Life"—there could be no other first topic in my senior course. If you see no possibility that life has any meaning, why bother discussing God, Faith, or Suffering at all? So that was where we started.

Friedrich Nietzsche and Overcoming Suffering

Friedrich Nietzsche's most well-known quote is "God is dead." Although Nietzsche died in 1900, the originator of nihilistic philosophy and the existentialist point of view still makes headlines, usually around Christmas or Easter. In 1966 an infamous *Time* magazine cover asked, "Is God Dead?" The cover became iconic as did the graffiti dialogue seen in bathrooms around the world: *God is dead*, signed Nietzsche; *Nietzsche is dead*, signed God. In the '60s a group of theologians claimed that the God of theism no longer made sense. They were referred to as "Death of God theologians," a provocative oxymoron if ever there was one!

Did Nietzsche believe that God had died? Nietzsche did not really concern himself with arguments for or against God's existence or subsequent demise. Nietzsche was reflecting on the concept of God and its power to provide meaning. Nietzsche wrote that organized Christianity had rendered God meaningless; the Christian concept of God was as empty as the churches themselves. Concerning Jesus, he went so far as to say that Christian leaders had perverted Jesus' teaching and twisted what was originally a message of love and acceptance into a message of fear and guilt. He called priests hypocrites, and churches "tombs and sepulchers" of a dead religion.[1] My students

---

[1] *The Gay Science*, Friedrich Nietzsche, Section 125.

really related to this. The charge of hypocrisy against authority figures is, of course, very popular with adolescents. And as my teaching years passed, the very public evidence of hypocrisy in Catholic leadership became increasingly difficult to avoid when these conversations occurred in the classroom.

But there was more to Nietzsche than his vitriol against organized Christianity. He reflected positively on the teaching of Jesus and Buddha. And although he didn't believe that there was any Ultimate Answer, any Divine Purpose or Plan, he did believe that we are free to choose our own. We are free to choose our personal goals and create our own meaning, and we have the power within us to achieve our chosen destiny. Neither the Church nor God had the power to determine our lives, just the Self. And this sense of personal power gave Nietzsche intense joy. It even brought him to tears, his biographers tell us.

A very subjective view of truth and meaning made sense to Nietzsche for personal reasons. He had struggled to extricate himself from his family's expectations that he become a Lutheran minister like his father, who had died when Nietzsche was very young. He had been burdened with a number of debilitating physical disorders: he suffered a major back injury while serving in the army and was crippled with pain for the rest of his life; he was plagued with migraines so severe they caused him to retire from university teaching at the age of 35 and seek relief in a circuit of health spas; he was rejected by two different women to whom he proposed marriage; he progressively lost both his sight and his mental stability, spending the last ten years of his life completely out of his mind. Immense pain and suffering coupled with his anger towards religion, and yet he never gave up looking for meaning and purpose. Despite so much being taken from him, he was determined to overcome it all and become the architect of his own destiny.

For the last ten years of his life, despite his declining health, he wrote prolifically and intensely about the ability of the human person to overcome suffering and imbue their lives with meaning. He denied himself painkillers for as long as he could, preferring the sharpness of his intellect while suffering pain to the dullness of his mind under the influence of drugs. You are probably familiar with two of his sayings about suffering:

> *He who has a why to live can bear with almost any how.*
> —Friedrich Nietzsche, *Twilight of the Idols*

In other words, if we can find a reason to live, we can bear with almost any suffering that comes our way. And even more famous,

> *That which does not kill us makes us stronger.*
> —Friedrich Nietzsche, *Twilight of the Idols*

For as long as his body and mind would allow him, Nietzsche fought to overcome his pain and suffering. The struggle made him stronger and gave him hope. He clutched at that hope until madness robbed him of his senses.

Hermann Hesse and the Universal Truths of Oneness and Love

Like Nietzsche, Hesse was a German Lutheran. Like Nietzsche, Hesse had a difficult childhood. His parents were demanding and controlling, continually rejected him for disobedience, sending him to foster families and boarding schools because he refused to be compliant and obedient. Hesse was a brilliant child who wrote poetry and painted, but his parents tried to force him to give up artistic pursuits. At 12 years of age when he declared that he wanted to be a poet, his parents sent him to a seminary boarding school, insisting that he become a Lutheran minister. He ran away. His parents even sent him to a mental institution for a time hoping to break his willfulness. Then at 15, he fell in love and was rejected. That was the last straw: he decided to commit suicide. He obtained a gun, left a suicide note, and ran away into the woods. He ultimately chose not to complete the act but never explained why. After this attempted suicide he took control of his life, quit school, left home, and eventually took a position working in a bookshop. Within a few years he was

a published poet and went on to become one of the most influential German authors of his generation.

Hesse survived his adolescence and overcame his childhood suffering, and for the rest of his life, like Nietzsche, he pursued his own meaning. Unlike Nietzsche, Hesse maintained a belief in God and as an adult became especially fascinated with Indian religions.

Hesse's ongoing struggles with depression and his attempt to get help through psychoanalysis inform his novels' main characters. Themes of internal conflict: desire versus duty; intellect versus passion; parental expectations versus adolescent rebellion, permeate his writings making them a rich resource for adolescent exploration, in particular. And his search for spiritual meaning is another common thread.

Hesse's novel, *Siddhartha*, about the life of a young Hindu man trying to decide what he wants to be and whose ideas he wants to follow, is thought to be based loosely on the life of the Buddha, Siddhartha Gautama. But it is also semiautobiographical. The book begins with the teenage Siddhartha rebelling against his father's expectations of him and setting out on his own: an archetypal story of growing up and one that has obvious parallels to Hesse's personal life.

In his own spiritual life Hesse's journey took him from Christianity to Buddhism and a lifelong fascination with India. In the novel *Siddhartha*, Hesse expresses a belief in the profound oneness of all reality and in the ultimate value of love.

> *"And everything together, all voices, all goals, all yearning, all suffering, all pleasure, all that was good and evil, all of this together was the world. All of it together was the flow of events, was the music of life."*
> —Hermann Hesse, *Siddhartha*

> *It seems to me, Govinda, that love is the most important thing in the world. It may be important to great thinkers to examine the world, to explain and*

despise it. But I think it is only important to love the world, not to despise it, not for us to hate each other, but to be able to regard the world and ourselves and all beings with love, admiration and respect."

> —Hermann Hesse, *Siddhartha*

Hesse was also a committed pacifist.

". . . I feel akin to you and to the idea that inspired the Nobel Foundation, the idea that the mind is international and supra-national, that it ought to serve not war and annihilation, but peace and reconciliation.

My ideal, however, is not the blurring of national characteristics, such as would lead to an intellectually uniform humanity. On the contrary, may diversity in all shapes and colours live long on this dear earth of ours. What a wonderful thing is the existence of many races, many peoples, many languages, and many varieties of attitude and outlook!"[2]

Viktor Frankl—Finding God and Meaning in a Concentration Camp

An Austrian psychotherapist and a Jew, Frankl lost his parents, his pregnant wife, and his brother in the concentration camps. Like all the Jews of his generation and since, Frankl struggled to reconcile the God of the Chosen People to the God of the Holocaust. God is One, and all things come from God. But how can this be? Perhaps, Frankl suggests, there isn't a single, ultimate answer. Perhaps instead, each of us has to give our own life meaning. This view is similar to the one expressed by Nietzsche, whom Frankl quotes in the opening of his book *Man's Search For Meaning*. But Frankl was neither an atheist nor a nihilist. Ironically Frankl's concentration camp experiences convinced him even more of the existence of God.

---

[2]"The Nobel Prize in Literature 1946, Banquet Speech," Hermann Hesse.
http://www.nobelprize.org/nobel_prizes/literature/laureates/1946/hesse-speech.html.

In the midst of the worst kind of evil that humans have ever enacted on other human beings, Frankl witnessed instances of self-sacrificing love and compassion. He saw people risk their own lives to give the dying a crust of bread, just to ease the pain of the dying one's last hours. For Frankl this was a sign of conscience and therefore of a God who is the source of conscience. Witnessing these acts gave Frankl hope in humanity's ability to overcome even the worst of trials.

Frankl also found meaning for his own life in the bunkhouses of Auschwitz. Using the tools of his profession, psychotherapy, he helped others find something to live for. He pointed out the smallest moments of grace and beauty in their torturous days; he encouraged individuals to gain strength from a memory of their spouse who would need them once they were released and who was depending on them to survive. Memories of his own wife and of her smile helped Frankl commit and recommit himself to surviving. Love was his salvation.

". . . A thought transfixed me: for the first time in my life I saw the truth as it is set into song by so many poets, proclaimed as the final wisdom by so many thinkers. The truth—that love is the ultimate and the highest goal to which man can aspire. Then I grasped the meaning of the greatest secret that human poetry and human thought and belief have to impart: The salvation of man is through love and in love. I understood how a man who has nothing left in this world may still know bliss, be it only for a brief moment, in the contemplation of his beloved. In a position of utter desolation, when a man cannot express himself in positive action, when his only achievement may consist in enduring his sufferings in the right way—an honorable way—in such a position man can, through loving contemplation of the image he carries of his beloved, achieve fulfillment. For the first time in my life, I was able to understand the words, 'The angels are lost in perpetual contemplation of an infinite glory.'"

—Viktor Frankl, *Man's Search For Meaning*

Mother Teresa's God—the God of all Faiths

An Albanian Catholic by the name of Agnes Gonxha Bojaxhiu became known to the world as Mother Teresa of Calcutta. As a teenager I had resisted learning about Mother Teresa, assuming that her story would be full of visions and saccharine piety and rosary beads. So I was delighted to discover the biography *The Simple Path* as an adult and learn that Mother Teresa was a Catholic very much in the spirit of Vatican II—she was open to the possibility that God hears all prayers not just Catholic ones. In fact Mother Teresa insisted that members of her order pray with the dying in the words of that person's faith, whether Hindu, Moslem, Sikh, or Christian. Unlike the over-zealous missionaries of the 19th century, Mother Teresa did not require Catholic Baptism of the sick before they would be offered nourishment and care in her homes for the dying.

Mother Teresa was the best of modern Catholicism, and she remains iconic in the Catholic Church. But faith was not easy for her. In letters published after her death, she describes feeling abandoned by God for decades. Her feeling of abandonment was in stark contrast to the spiritual intimacy she had experienced early in her religious life, making the loss of God later in life even more debilitating. Some modern commentators have suggested that her faith struggle makes her a poor model for Catholics. I think it makes her an even better one. Think of the courage it took to keep going in her ministry day after day, year after year. People looked up to her as a spiritual icon, and yet in her prayer she no longer felt God's presence just an emptiness, a loss, an ache for something that once was. Here was a realistic role model for young people trying to understand faith: faith isn't easy, and "feeling" the presence of God may not be part of the package, at least not all the time. Faith is a decision that, like commitment in a marriage, has to be made over and over.

Perhaps it was her own "dark night of the soul" that made Mother Teresa more appreciative of other people's faith journeys. Who was she to deny the presence of God in someone else's life, or to deny the validity of a religious path other than Catholicism? It was this openness to other world faiths that made Mother Teresa so inspiring to me.

"There is only one God and He is God to all; therefore it is important that everyone is seen as equal before God. I've always said we should help a Hindu become a better Hindu, a Muslim become a better Muslim, a Catholic become a better Catholic. We believe our work should be our example to people. We have among us 475 souls—30 families are Catholics and the rest are all Hindus, Muslims, Sikhs—all different religions. But they all come to our prayers."

"There are so many religions and each one has its different ways of following God. I follow Christ."

—Mother Teresa, *The Simple Path*

I am not a great advocate of rote memorization, but I encouraged my seniors to memorize the following poem. I admit, I may have offered bonus points on the test. But I felt it is worthy of remembering. It contains a whole philosophy of life without any doctrine or even any answers. It offers more than that: it is a way to live that can make it all bearable, even beautiful. One of my students nicknamed it the "fruit prayer." Sometimes we would recite it together as our opening prayer before class.

The Simple Path
"The fruit of silence is prayer,
the fruit of prayer is faith,
the fruit of faith is love,
the fruit of love is service,
the fruit of service is peace."
—Mother Teresa, *The Simple Path*

My teaching was coinciding with my life. I was searching for meaning, especially meaning in suffering. My students and the senior course sustained me. Even as I faltered in my commitment to the Church, I felt stronger in my personal faith than I had for a number of years. I was working with retreats and leading liturgical music for school masses and celebrations. I even wrote a song for the school to use at the groundbreaking ceremony for a new building.

> *"If God is our cornerstone, if God is our whole life's foundation,*
> *If God is our cornerstone, we will rise."*
> —"The Cornerstone" by Mona Villarrubia

The faith expressed in this song was genuine. God truly was the cornerstone of my life. Maybe this period of renewal was God or the Universe preparing me for what was to happen. Maybe. Sometimes I'd like to think so.

LOSING MY RELIGION

The Sexual Abuse Crisis of 2002 and its impact on my life and faith.

My Personal Sexual Abuse Crisis

What was the "Sexual Abuse Crisis" exactly? It was not, as many may assume, the fact that there were child abusers in the Catholic priesthood. Child abuse is a horrific crime, but it is sadly a statistical probability that there are child abusers in every neighborhood, every school system, every religion, and in every level of leadership within that religion. So the presence of abusers among Catholic clergy was not in itself a sudden revelation or crisis. The crisis for Catholics that occurred in the early 2000s was, in my opinion, more of a crisis of trust brought about by the revelation of a cover-up—an organized, systematic, cover-up.

As a child victim of sexual assault by two Catholic priests, the sexual abuse crisis is not just a national crisis it is a personal matter. I don't know when my abuse began exactly, but I remember knowing I was being abused by the age of 6. How long before that it did it start? I don't know. But it one memory that has bothered me forever, I am being led by the hand of a woman into a priest's office. I was wearing training pants which suggests my age was around three. My small height in that memory—not reaching as far up as the woman's hip—would also support that age. This memory has always felt ominous, but until recently the memory stopped as soon as the priest stood up from behind his desk and started towards me. It is only in the past few years that the memory has begun to unwrap. Memory fragments consisting of smells, body sensations, taste, intrusive images and thoughts, and more recently some intense flashbacks, have added to the memory of that scene.

I have always remembered certain instances of abuse. The memory of my first experience of sexual pleasure while sitting on a priest's lap with his fingers in my underpants is seared into my memory forever, as is the feeling of shame. But I have struggled to accept the sometimes partial nature of other memories. It has helped that my two older brothers have affirmed many pieces of those memories and have sadly admitted their own abuse by the same two priests. What is most tragic, and hardest to comprehend on so many levels, is what our parents revealed in their last few years of life: they had been sexually victimized by the very same two priests. My father since early adolescence, my mother as an adult. These priests were friends to each other and acted as each other's confessor. The priests controlled and intimidated our parents throughout their dating and the early years of their marriage, and the priests shared access to us, the children.

I cannot begin to put into words the anger these revelations have caused. How could our parents have allowed access to their children, having themselves been sexually assaulted by these two men. The psychology of victimization could shed some light I'm sure, but not enough to dissolve the anger we all have been left to process.

So much abuse. Yet in the 1980s and '90s neither my abuse nor the growing awareness of my brothers' abuse caused me to lose my trust in the Catholic Church. The two priests who damaged us so badly were evil individuals who happened to share a predilection for children. They did not represent the whole Church, so I did not hold the whole Church responsible. In fact, it was my faith in God and my love of the Church that had kept me going as a teenager and had inspired me to pursue a career in religious education. I wanted to share my faith with teenagers who were struggling to find meaning in their suffering, just as I had struggled. In a very real sense my experience of abuse provided me with a vocation. And the development of my senior course was a direct response to this sense of vocation.

Clearly, for me then, the abuse crisis was not a crisis brought on by the sudden awareness of abusive clergy. It was, as I have said above, a crisis of trust.

And I believe the same is true for many other Catholics. The issue for us was not the existence of clergy predators; it was the revelation of an enabling and duplicitous organization.

The Loss of my Guardian Angel

My sexual abuse by priests had not caused me to lose my faith in God or the Church, but there had been losses along the way. When I was a child I lost my guardian angel.

> *Dear God,*
>
> *I know you are my Father and you love me, and I know you only punish me when I deserve it, but I don't understand. Why have you taken away my angel? Mummy says we all have guardian angels, and she showed me a picture of one in my storybook. My angel is so beautiful with big soft white wings. I think about her standing over my bed, and then I can go to sleep and not be scared.*
>
> *But that was before. Now I feel scared every night. And I have really bad dreams where someone's arms come out of the wall above my bed and reach down and grab me. I get a really bad pain in my middle like a hot poker is being stuck into my tummy. Then I feel sick.*
>
> *Did I do something really, really bad that made you mad at me? I'm sorry if I did. If I say my prayers every day and promise to be a good girl and help mummy, can I have my guardian angel back? Please? I just don't want to be scared at night any more.*

When I was a child I had the traditional image of God as a heavenly Father. Like most children, my image of God was drawn from my experience of my own father combined with pictures in religious story books and prayers I was taught to say. All this was mixed up with my experience of priests, our other "fathers." I believed that when I was old enough to go to confession, the priest

would tell God all the bad things I did. To my child's mind priests were like Santa's helpers, and God kept the "list" and checked it at least twice.

There was a prayer I said every night:

Now I lay me down to sleep,
I pray you Lord my soul to keep.
Angels guard me through the night,
And keep me safe 'til morning light.

This prayer was important to me. I probably said it out of a mixture of fear and piety. Fear that if I didn't say it something bad would happen, and piety because the pictures of beautiful angels in my storybooks made me feel good about praying. Also the statue of Mary on my chest-of- drawers made me feel special—I wanted to be loved by that beautiful lady and fly with the angels.

My father was a distant, authoritarian figure, and so was my God. God had all the power and knew everything I did and, like my dad, God knew when any of us deserved punishment, and his anger was loud and physical. God knew everything, I believed. So, when bad things happened at night, God must have known and must have allowed it to happen. I was being punished but I didn't know what for. Whatever it was, though, it must have been really bad because God had taken away my guardian angel.

I remember vividly the sadness I felt, and I can still recall the recurrent nightmares. I knew I must be bad, but part of me clung tenaciously to the hope that praying and being good would earn me back my guardian angel. If I made my First Communion and First Confession, surely I would be holy then? And God would let me start over? Wouldn't he?

My sexual abuse by Catholic priests did not cause me to doubt the existence of God or the truth of my religion, or like C.S. Lewis to doubt the goodness of God. Instead it caused me to lose faith in my own goodness. They say it is easier for a child to believe she is responsible for her abuse than to believe that adults, especially parents and parent-figures, cannot be trusted, because if this were true then the whole world was unsafe, and that possibility is just too overwhelming for a child to accept. Ironically, it was this self-blame that helped me to hold on to my faith. If I was to blame, God wasn't. I deserved to be punished because I was bad; God was just and, hopefully, merciful.

In the late 1990s the possibility of institutionalized evil in the Catholic Church was still too overwhelming for me to consider. If it was true that abuse was widespread and had been condoned, or at the very least covered up, my whole life would have to change—my career, my religion, my music ministry. I wasn't ready for that. I was going to hold on for dear life to my life as it was, for as long as I possibly could. I told myself the abuse of my family was a personal issue and did not require an indictment of the whole Church. I committed myself even more to helping students find meaning and purpose in their lives and in their faith, and I committed myself to the continued pursuit of personal healing. This attitude of denial worked for a while. But then Boston happened.

Boston 2002

The Catholic Church's mishandling of the problem of sexually abusive priests became a daily news headline in 2002. I was in Europe that summer, and while I was there I had a meltdown. Too many churches, monasteries, statues, strange bedrooms, and one horrible flashback or hallucination of an old man in black sitting on the corner of my bed, masturbating. Not only did I "see" him, I also smelled him. I spent the rest of the night curled up in the shower stall in my room.

The next day I made an international call to my therapist and asked if I could sign up again; it had been a few years. She referred me to someone else. I was a bit too much of a commitment for her; she was only working part-time, and she felt that given what was coming up I needed a trauma specialist. So I came back from that trip, found a new therapist—a specialist in sexual trauma—and published my first article on being abused by a Catholic priest, "Forgive and Forget?" It was published in the Jesuit journal, *America Magazine*, and I was terrified.

I was a Catholic theology teacher in a Catholic High School. I had just published an article identifying myself as a victim of sexual abuse by a priest, a victim who wasn't sure how to move forward with her church. But my fears of negative fallout at work proved unfounded. I received only support and sympathy from my Dominican peers. My students, on the other hand, weren't likely to read the Jesuit journal, and I certainly wasn't going to bring it to their attention.

I knew that the Catholic Church wasn't perfect, but that didn't mean I couldn't defend it. Any cursory historical survey reveals egregious moral and intellectual errors: the inquisition, anti-Semitism, ecclesial corruption, the rejection of science, misogyny. But one of the reasons I loved the Catholic Church and chose to become a theology teacher was its willingness (in the second half of the 20th century) to admit its errors and make changes in its teaching. I had proudly defended a church that was open to such growth. I still believed I would see a married priesthood and female clergy in my lifetime. As long as the Church was committed to dealing with the sexual abuse issue, I argued to myself, I could continue to support it. And so, in the early years of the 21st century I still remained faithful, and I was convinced that the American bishops, now that they had been "found out," would do the right thing.

In the spring of 2002 I joined a support group for survivors of sexual abuse by Catholic Priests—SNAP (Survivors Network of those Abused by Priests and Religious). We told our stories, offered each other support, and planned leafleting, public demonstrations, and activism. We worked with a lawyer to petition the state to extend the statute of limitations on sexual abuse. The public events felt empowering but also terrifying and completely overwhelming. "Overwhelmed" was a constant state of being in those months. At a candlelight vigil for abuse victims who had committed suicide, I felt like I was drowning. It was cold and windy, and the cold seemed to move inside. A friend asked if I was okay. I just looked at him and said, "I don't know."

Some people hear stories of priests who have abused children and refuse to believe it; some victims hear stories of a Church who cares about them and refuse to believe it. And some victims would rather die than have to tell their story again to lawyers and priests and psychiatrists who dismiss their pain and try to talk them out of their truth. SNAP meetings were a safe place to share our stories; we were always believed, always supported, and that felt good. But the stories of other people's abuse were hard to listen to, week after week. And still the membership kept growing.

The Charter—A Sign of Hope?

In 2002 it seemed to me that, amidst all the horror stories of abuse and cover-up that were emerging, there was a sign of hope. The United States Conference of Catholic Bishops (USCCB) produced *"The Charter for the Protection of Children and Young People."* This *Charter* was a major development, and involved some reluctant eating of crow by the American hierarchy. Lay advisory boards were established in each diocese with the purpose of reviewing sexual abuse allegations. I was invited to sit on our review board in New Orleans, and also on the Dominican review board for the southern province. An independent firm was hired to train the Dominican review board members, oversee investigations, and draw up proposals of care. No training was offered by the diocese, but it was a step in the right direction. I was the only abuse victim on both boards, and I felt a responsibility to "represent."

In the classroom, students who asked about the abuse crisis received an honest but nonpersonal response that horrible mistakes had been made by our church leaders. I pointed out that the *Charter* was a sign of change, a new commitment to transparency and to justice for the victims and their families going forward. I didn't just teach it, I believed it. I was wrong. But I didn't know how wrong.

Confronting the Contradictions

Following is a journal entry on the conflicted emotions I was feeling in the light of the sex abuse crisis that I wrote in the Spring of 2002.

"I can't decide if I am the awed child in front of the stained glass windows lighting a candle, the depressed teenager searching for someone to love, the grateful parent, the dedicated religion teacher, the enthused liturgical musician, or the angry abuse victim. I can't decide because I am all of them. I would feel as dishonest denying my enthused liturgical musician-self to please my angry SNAP friends, as I would denying my angry abused victim-self to my co-workers and employers in order to make my job more secure.

Despite the obvious contradictions, I am both angry with and yet still involved in the Catholic Church. That is the daily truth I live with and in so doing I make a lot of people feel uncomfortable. But I have come to terms with my situation and have made my own compromises. I have decided that simply staying angry merely fuels the feelings of hopelessness and helplessness that all victims feel when faced with the Church bureaucracy. A more constructive position is to support efforts of communication between victims and the Church. Whether confrontational or conciliatory, dialogue is better than stagnating in one's anger."

From 2002 to 2004 I continued teaching my course, leading my department, giving occasional talks on the abuse issue and holding my Catholicism together.

From Hurt to Healing

When my book, *From Hurt to Healing*, came out in 2004 and was reviewed in the *New Orleans Times Picayune*, it was harder to avoid public awareness. My pained-looking face figured prominently in the press release, with a dramatic background of religious art. The picture was taken in my foyer, where I have a collection of contemporary Christian folk art from South America. Colorful, vibrant figures of Noah and the animals, the last supper, and the risen Jesus, adorn my green walls and greet you as you enter my house. What can I say;

I am (was) a religious geek. That's exactly what the photo represented—my religious ambivalence: am/was.

Luckily, most teenagers don't read newspapers any more than they read theology journals, but their parents do. And they did. Happily, I was very touched by the tenderness and tact that people showed me—parents, teachers, administrators, even the school's Board of Directors. Those few students who discovered the book never asked me about it in front of others, always outside of class. People respected my decision to publish, and my commitment not to discuss personal issues in school. And that meant I could continue to teach, at least for a while.

My husband suggests occasionally, and gently, that maybe I could be just a little less honest, a little less forthcoming, a little less vivid. He has had to put up with so much from me that maybe I should heed his request more. But I don't. And, despite my going on public record about my sexual dysfunction and struggles with depression, he stands by me. Always and ever, he is my rock. He's kind of grey and craggy looking like a rock, too, but I love him more now than I did when we married. And apparently he must love me, too. Why else would he have stuck with me through all this. A good man. A righteous man. Not a saint, though . . . thank God! I couldn't have survived being married to a saint (or someone who thought he was).

After the article I was pleasantly surprised by requests to give talks and have book signings. My parish priest invited me to do a reading and book signing in the parish center. The Archbishop reviewed and accepted my book and continued to support my position as a religious educator. The local Catholic community I belonged to was defending me, but my commitment to defending my church was wearing thin.

Katrina interrupted everything in the fall of 2005. I didn't have the time and energy to keep up with all the abuse allegations that continued to surface in the news, and activism was out of the question: our group was spread all over the country. I was just trying to figure out how and where to get laundry done and how many varieties of crock-pot casseroles I could create, and how

in heaven's name to prepare for Christmas. Were we even going to be home by then?

My sexual abuse issues didn't go away; they were just sidelined for a few months. I didn't have to face any career changing decisions because my school was under water, and we wouldn't be back for a whole semester. Once we returned I simply kept going. Treading water! The lake had receded back to its regular boundaries beyond the levees, but the church hierarchy was getting ready to release another tsunami of indefensible behavior that would drown my Catholic faith. I would no longer be able to defend my church.

Being the Victim of Abuse by a Priest Means . . .

- deciding as a child that I must be a bad girl because God has taken away my guardian angel
- being afraid of old men's hands
- having an orgasm before I knew what that meant
- not being able to breathe suddenly, when I see a man in a black suit and clerical collar
- having a panic attack when I walk into a church at the age of 47
- going to a parish Mass in 2004 and bursting into tears during the Our Father, when it says "as we forgive those" because I know I haven't forgiven my church yet and I don't know if I can
- feeling revictimized by the lies and coverups orchestrated by my bishops
- finally losing my religion after years of devotion to my church
- missing the beauty and solace of the sacraments
- longing for the serenity and safety I had always felt in a church or chapel
- mourning the loss of my church

Two Types of Abuser Priests That I Have Known

The "buddy" priest.

There seem to be two very different types of priest-predators. First there is the type of pedophile-priest who is stuck in emotional and psychological adolescence, who bonds really well with children, appears to love them and understand them, and wants to work with them. This type of predator attracts children to him because he shows them lots of attention; they are often children from emotionally damaged homes, broken marriages, or abusive parents. They crave affection and attention and long to feel special; they love being loved. They also enjoy the hero worship of prepubescent children. This kind of abuser seeks out such children and can spend years grooming them before sexual contact is initiated. He doesn't have to rush because he is already actively abusing other children. He has the opportunity to build layers of trust and confidentiality and "special" bonding before he tests that trust with a sexual advance: a backrub, naked swimming, wrestling, sharing confidences, sharing a bed.

The buddy priest does not get along well with his peers, who may worry about his boundary issues. They probably don't voice their concerns to anyone except their fellow priests, though, with whom the pedophile's success with children becomes the subject of dinner table jokes. Parents trust this type of pedophile-priest because he shows their kids so much attention and seems to be having such a good influence on them. He gets kids interested in being altar boys or in the boy scouts and camping. And that is great, because the parents just don't have the time for all of that. Even more so (especially in the past), parents were grateful for the priest's nurturing of their son's vocation to the priesthood, encouraging his devotion to the Church.

Thanks, Father! Maybe you can get Jordan to think about his future. He needs a good education, huh, Father. Maybe a scholarship to a good high school. You could help with that, Father? Put in a good word? Be nice to Father, Jordan, he can help you. A camping trip to the lake? Great idea, Father. Be good for the boys. Get them out of the city, away from the damn TV.

Catholics in my parents' generation put priests on pedestals and offered them their children without question for mentoring, field trips, camping, and vacations. As a teenager my father was sent off by my grandparents to be the summer vacation driver for a priest—a family friend. This family friend became his abuser and later his stalker and finally his adult lover.

The charismatic priest.

Secondly there is the type of priest-predator who is described as a charismatic leader, ambitious, one who gathers Catholic leadership around him and "gets things done." He opens a new parish, builds a new school, pays off the parish debt in an efficient and record-breaking campaign. He's a man's man with tastes in expensive single malts, season tickets to the NFL, good cars, and only the best restaurants. He likes the idea of becoming a Monsignor, but he might not want to leave his parish, he's invested too much time lining his nest.

This second type flirts publicly with women, and privately with men. He is a sexual predator whose prey often involves the young and vulnerable, people he can control through intimidation because of his position in the Church. He is an opportunist, a predator of convenience: whoever is in his sights and can be had. It might be prepubescent girls or boys, the children of friends and family members, troubled college students who have sought him out for counseling, seminarians struggling with their vocation, or young wives in difficult marriages. Anyone he can exert power and control over, anyone who looks up to him, anyone in awe of his status, anyone whose life he could make difficult if they spoke up.

The sexual gratification he receives is as much about power as it is about lust. He probably lives a lifestyle that is not that of a typical parish priest, indulging in luxuries that sometimes raise eyebrows but can always be argued away by saying it comes from private gifts or a personal inheritance. He would never have chosen to join a religious order and taken a vow of poverty; he was always interested in advancement and promotion. One day he will make a good bishop, as long as he can keep his peccadilloes to a minimum and keeps raising lots of money. Hopefully, he will never get caught with a child; and if any victims come forward later in life, his status in the church by then will make him a powerful force to contend with publicly. He may even get a promotion and reassignment from his bishop just to keep everything quiet.

If the charismatic priest belongs to a religious order, his personal life-style is excused as the necessary trappings of a leader and fundraiser who needs to hold his own in society with those who have power and money. He is an intellectual, with knowledge of the arts and fine wines. He makes a great Provincial or University President.

This type of priest benefits especially from the medieval view of the priesthood that has enjoyed a recent resurgence. According to medieval theology (supported in recent times by Popes John Paul II and Benedict XVI) priests at ordination experience an ontological change: the very quality of their humanness is raised to a different level, "a humanity more closely united to the one Christ" to quote a document on the Vatican web site, "Priests in the Early Church and in Vatican II." The Catholic Church cannot heal from the sexual abuse crisis if it continues to maintain this archaic, misguided theology of priesthood.

Of the two types of predator-priest I have outlined, can you guess which ends up in litigation? I expect none of the second type have ever served time in jail. In fact, if you think about it just a little, you can probably name at least one priest whose sexual improprieties not only didn't land him in jail but actually resulted in a promotion or a comfortable retirement. The founder of the Legionaries of Christ is the most egregious example of this type of sex-abuser priest, raping under-age boys as well as seminarians, and having families with two different common-law wives.

Catholic Guilt; Catholic Shame

Guilt and shame; staples of a Catholic education in the '50s and early '60s; the very foundation of Catholic moral instruction, especially in the area of human sexuality. So how is it that the pedophile priests themselves did not seem to feel the guilt and shame they preached?

Young boys were tormented by priests with threats of hell if they masturbated, but chasing altar boys was the topic of dinner time jokes in seminaries and rectories. For teenage boys touching yourself was a shameful and guilt-ridden exercise in self-damnation; but for priests, touching young boys was an exercise in power and control.

What about when the priests were accused? The boy victims were beaten by their fathers or by another "Father." *"How could you say such lies? You are going to hell for such sins."* And the pedophiles were told by their bishops *"We will pray for you, my son, that you can overcome this temptation from the devil. Remember he strikes hardest at the holiest among us."* Pedophile priests were to be pitied. Their struggle was an indication of their inherent holiness! If young boys "gave in" and "allowed" themselves to be touched, that was a sign that they were agents of the devil. The shame and guilt was the boys. My own father was called a deviant and took a beating when he tried to tell his dad about the abuse.

It doesn't seem that the Catholic Church has come very far on this issue. Victims who come forward become the problem. And there is still a lack of shame and guilt on the part of the pedophile priests and their bishops. The priests may be more likely viewed as sad victims of a disordered sexuality than as the target of the devil's temptation, but bishops continue to protect and defend them. And so many bishops exhibit little to no compassion for the young children molested, raped, and sodomized by members of their clergy.

The burden of shame and guilt carried by victims is immense. I have spent years trying to move out of a position of shame, even though it was never my shame to bear. And now I recognize that nothing will change in the treatment of victims in the Church unless the criminal priests and their enabling bishops are made to accept the shame and guilt as theirs.

The Final Disillusionment

In June of 2002, the U.S. Bishops adopted the *Charter for the Protection of Children and Young People*. The *Charter* adopted a "one strike" policy with regard to priests serving in any active, public ministry. The *Charter* called for the institution of lay advisory boards in each diocese to advise bishops on the credibility of abuse accusations. A revised *Charter* was approved by the full body of U.S. Catholic bishops (USCCB) at its June 2005 General Meeting.

In 2004, Cardinal Francis George, acting as vice-president of the USCCB, lead a delegation of bishops to the Vatican to discuss changing church laws that hold bishops accountable to the *Charter*. He then hosted a summit of the nation's bishops in Chicago to finalize revisions to the *Charter*. However, it came to light that, in his role as Archbishop of Chicago, Cardinal George had completely ignored this very same *Charter* and overruled his own advisory board.

In the fall of 2005 a priest in Chicago was arrested for the sexual abuse of a child. He was released. The review board discovered a track record of abuse allegations going back more than eleven years and recommended his immediate removal from ministry pending further internal investigation. Ignoring the recommendations of his own advisory board, which were in compliance with the norms he had helped to write in the *Charter*, Cardinal George chose to protect this priest. The priest was reassigned by George, and over the next twelve months went on to abuse at least four more boys. The priest was finally removed in 2006, put on trial, and sent to jail for five years.

This case took my breath away. I had had such hopes for the *Charter*, and I had trusted Cardinal George. In April I wrote a letter to the editor of the *National Catholic Reporter*.

Regarding your editorial "A request to Cardinal George" (NCR, March 31, 2006):

The recent revelations concerning Cardinal Francis George, a man who had given the appearance of truly wanting to make a difference, have been harder for me to swallow than the national abuse reports. Why? Because after all those awful revelations I was desperate for a sign of hope in our church and I chose to believe in him. I trusted him; I thought he was a man of integrity, a sign of grace. But Cardinal George has knowingly disregarded the very Charter he helped formulate. A priest under his charge, Fr. Daniel McCormack, was still in active service despite a record of accusations of sexual misconduct going back

14 years. And although he was again accused of sexual abuse in August 2005, Cardinal George overruled his own review board in allowing McCormack to remain in active and, to all intents and purposes, unsupervised ministry with young boys. Did he warn the parents in the parish? No. But now Cardinal George wants to "take responsibility?" I don't know what that means. Apparently, for George, being responsible doesn't mean doing the right thing; it means only saying or writing the right things and apologizing when you are caught not living up to it.

—*National Catholic Reporter*, April 28, 2006

The behavior of Cardinal George was the final straw for me. I was done trying to defend the indefensible. I had lost my religion. In the same month that I wrote this letter, I gave in my resignation; I was done teaching Catholic theology. I didn't have another job or another plan. I had reached the proverbial knot at the end of my rope, and it hadn't held. Even without the stress of a semester recovering from Katrina I would have reached the same conclusion: I had lost my religion, and I could no longer work for the Church.

Shock, Suffering . . . Recovery?

There is another version of the stages of grieving that I have come across that is simpler than Kübler-Ross's theory described earlier. It identifies only three stages: Shock, Suffering, Recovery. I like the simplicity of this. These stages might mask the complexity of grief, but they make it possible for me to reflect on the loss of my religion without complete overwhelm. And, unlike Kübler-Ross's theory, they naturally follow each other.

Shock

How could the truth about some of the bishops of my Church have been a shock? How could I still have faith in a religious organization that had consistently and repeatedly let me down by not protecting me from known abusers? One of the priests who abused me and members of my family had such an egregious reputation in his own religious community that he and his biological brother (also a member of the same order) were described by a fellow religious as profoundly evil men.

Nonetheless, it was a shock because I had managed to separate my abuse from my experience of the rest of the Church. The same Catholic Church that protected my abusers had also protected me and nurtured me and educated me. The best people I knew were Catholic; the only people who had ever cared about me were Catholic, some of them were priests and nuns. My powers of denial were great, and my need to trust my Church was even greater. So, yes, when Cardinal George proved to be a hypocrite and revealed his own cynical disregard for innocent children, I was shocked. Shocked and sickened.

I had defended my Church to other victims. I had defended my job as a Catholic educator to the national survivors group, SNAP. I felt stupid, naïve, gullible. I felt as if I had been abused all over again on some level because the shock left me exposed and vulnerable. And it left me angry and afraid. What was I going to do? Who was I going to be?

Suffering

Anger and fear are part of the second stage. Once the initial shock of grief wears off, you begin to connect to your emotions—intense, confused, overwhelming emotions. I was so angry, at myself first and foremost. How had I continued defending my Church knowing what I had known since 2002? But I had. I had repeatedly defended it to myself, to my students, and to other victims. I felt guilty and ashamed, as if I had been complicit in the coverups, in the lies, and in the hypocrisy. Remaining a teacher of theology in a Catholic school would make me a knowing enabler of what now seemed to me to be a corrupt and abusive system. I had been naïve long enough, always believing the best, hoping for change, looking for signs of justice. I felt foolish, embarrassed by my gullibility, and so very, very angry. Even if I had wanted to continue in the classroom, I wouldn't have lasted long. Hiding emotions has never been a talent of mine; my students would have read my face and "heard" what

it was that I wasn't saying. Cynicism would have eaten its way into my humor; it was already beginning to. My students deserved better than that.

Fear held me back from turning in my resignation for a few months. I couldn't imagine doing anything other than teaching, and there was no room in public schools for theology teachers. I was convinced that there was nothing else I could do other than go into retail sales. It didn't help that I had for most of my life thought of myself as less than gifted to say the least. Falling in love with someone in college who was on his third degree while I was just working on my first had not helped my academic self-confidence any. It wasn't until I received my master's degree that I began to really internalize the fact that I was quite intelligent, maybe even talented in some ways. Now the thought of leaving education brought back all my old insecurities. What could I actually do other than teach?

Being a victim and also an educator in the Catholic Church had been like living in a house at the top of a cliff. For years the edge of my cliff had been eroding, the margin of safety getting slimmer and slimmer. Then one day I woke up and walked out the door and, without expecting it, I fell off the cliff. I was free-falling, and I couldn't catch my breath. As I looked back, I could see people painting a white picket fence on the walls of the house, trying to give the illusion to passers by that it was still safe. I saw many, many people clambering up the cliff face trying to reach the house, believing it could still provide shelter from the storm, believing in the painted fence, the illusion of safety. But I felt differently now, and it felt like I was dying.

Somewhere on the way down to the bottom of the cliff I discovered that I could fly and then I knew I would survive. Just a metaphor, I know . . . the house and the cliff. And I know I can't fly. When I was a little girl and suffered from recurrent nightmares of being chased by people trying to kill me, I would sometimes dream that I could fly. As if by the power of my will I could raise my body off the ground and escape the evil that was seeking me out. Sometimes I only managed to raise myself off the ground a little; other times I was able to soar above the rooftops and trees. Those were wonderful dreams. But back in reality in 2006 I was not "flying" above the abuse crisis, I was simply managing not to crash against the rocks.

I couldn't in all honesty encourage fidelity to an institution whose leaders had proved again and again to be callously indifferent to its children. I had made excuses for too long, "The bishops couldn't have known a priest would abuse again." But they could and did, because it kept happening with appalling frequency, in diocese after diocese. The bishops of the United States had been warned about the scope of the problem in a document written in 1985 by Rev. Tom Doyle, OP, JCD; F. Ray Mouton, JD; and Rev. Michael Peterson, MD. The document was presented to the annual Bishops Meeting of the National Council of Catholic Bishops. It was then copied and sent to every diocese in the country and to the Bishops Council. Later, many bishops would deny ever having received it.

Another issue for me was the growing number of suicides among Catholic victims who had come forward only to feel revictimized by the adversarial and litigious behavior of their dioceses. I lost one of my own friends that way. So I gave in my notice at work. I was done with the Catholic Church. But what would I do now? I felt rudderless. This is where the experience in Houston was such a gift: I knew I could work successfully in an office environment.

Although I was ready to leave Catholic education, I couldn't give up the idea of working for a religious institution. I wanted, I needed, a group of people who cared about "ultimate things" and about God. Ironically, I still felt safer working in a faith community. It was as if the rest of the world couldn't be trusted not to hurt me. Even though I had experienced life-shattering trauma in the Catholic Church, I still felt, and feel, that people who commit their lives to God are mainly good and caring people. I wanted to work for people who worked for God. Sound pious? Maybe even pretentious? Perhaps. Maybe it was just the scared child in me dreaming of a safe home.

The first job I applied for advertised a "stress free" work environment. That ended up being false advertising, but what I discovered was a great group of people committed to social justice and concerned about their religious

identity: I found a job at a Reform Synagogue. It would become my professional and spiritual home for seven years.

Professionally, I had found a way to move on, but on a personal level I was just beginning to grieve the loss of my religion. Passing a Church building caused emotional and even physical reactions. Sadness and anger all mixed up in a shame soup with a side order of guilt. It was a good thing that my sons were both young adults and separate enough from me not to be offended by my rejection of the Church. They were already on their own particular quests for meaning and self-hood and didn't talk about religion much.

My sons would be okay, but I was overwhelmed by a sense of guilt concerning my students. For 27 years I had taught high school theology to about 150 students each year. That's a lot of students. I really didn't want to offend them or hurt their faith in the Church or more importantly in God. Would they think I had lied to them? That it was all a sham on my part? I kept telling myself over and over: You have done nothing wrong. You are the victim, not the perpetrator. You have struggled to remain honest and to keep your integrity. What could I do to their faith that the bishops hadn't already done? But I still felt as if I had let them all down.

If you suffer sexual abuse by a priest or religious, you suffer the loss of much more than your physical and psychological wholeness. Not only is your body violated and your sense of safety destroyed, you have your faith brutalized. For Catholic abuse victims our church doesn't feel safe; it probably isn't even welcoming any more if we have gone public. Some of us find other faith communities. I had taken a job in a Jewish Synagogue and attended services there on occasion, but I still considered myself Catholic. I just wasn't sure what that meant or what I wanted it to mean to me.

Recovery

As soon as I started my new job, I immersed myself in Reform Judaism. I tried once again (I had tried as a teacher years before) to learn Hebrew, and with about the same degree of success—not much. I borrowed books from the library, and I read excerpts from the most recent edition of the Reform prayer book, the *Mishkan T'fillah*. This was me doing recovery: putting my faith back together using different-shaped bricks, maybe, but bricks made from the same clay. I attended a few services and felt like an outsider. Not because of the people there but because I couldn't share in the prayers. Even the transliterations of the Hebrew prayers were tough to follow at first. Many of their prayers are in English, though, and having a good ear for music I was able to join in some of the choruses of the sung prayers. I have since learned that many Jews in my age group in the Reform movement had not grown up learning Hebrew. The use of Hebrew was initially rejected by the Reform movement and then later brought back, rather like the use of Latin following Vatican II. So I was in good company.

Although graciously welcomed by my new Jewish community, I felt like an unfaithful lover. And I missed the contemporary Christian music I used to sing. So when I was invited to play guitar at an interfaith thanksgiving service hosted by the synagogue, I jumped at the chance, and invited some students from my old school. That was a great experience, but it made me nostalgic for my liturgical music group at Dominican. Had I made the right decision? Had it been pride of some kind that made me quit my teaching job in the Catholic system? Couldn't I just fudge a bit on the contract where it asked if you were a practicing Catholic "in good standing" with the Church. Oh, it was very tempting. Who would know that I wasn't attending parish mass any more? As the spring rolled around and contract discussions were underway again across the Archdiocese, I began to toy with the idea of going back to teaching. But as I rehearsed an interview in my head, I found couldn't bring myself to lie. The Bishops of the American Catholic Church were not defensible; I would not defend them, and I could not in good conscience ask students to support them or support the Church. It became clearer and clearer: I could not go back to teaching Catholic theology, not now, maybe not ever. Having a reasonably well-paying job gave me the luxury of making a decision according to conscience. I considered myself lucky, even blessed, to have that option.

The synagogue provided a shelter at a time when the Catholic Church no longer offered me succor. I began to reach into the heart of modern Judaism in search of God and of a spiritual home. Reform Judaism has a wonderful vision of social justice and ecological responsibility. They are committed to *tikkun olam* which means the healing of the world. The religious education program has three pillars: the study of Torah, participation in Worship, and Social Action or Acts of Loving Kindness. I could commit to such an educational program: children learning hands-on that serving others is part of their religious tradition.

But there was always something lacking; there were words that were never used: Faith, Ministry, Vocation, Prayer. Prayers, yes, but prayer—the personal relationship with the Holy—not as much. Even the word God was rarely invoked and not because of a religious proscription but rather a desire not to make those synagogue members feel uncomfortable who weren't sure about the meaning of the term or the existence of a corresponding reality.

It seemed that, theologically speaking, Reform Judaism sometimes had more in common with secular humanism than theism. I missed God. And the services, while beautiful, were a strange combination of the archaic Hebrew language which very, very few members actually understood, and modern prose; ancient melodies and modern guitar arrangements. I missed those moments at services when you directly address God, in the faith that God is indeed among you. I missed prayer.

And then, the most archaic of all traditions is how they use the Torah, their sacred five books. There is Torah study on the Sabbath for those who wish to read and discuss the passage of the week in English. But if you attend services you will hear the Hebrew intoned from the sacred Torah Scroll. No translation is offered in the service book; people are not encouraged to bring a copy of the Torah in English. It is up to the Rabbi to sermonize and relate the story to the congregation. The most important part of the service and no one knows what it says. I missed the Bible.

Judaism offered a faith community and a sacred calendar around which to order my life. But it wasn't going to be a long-term solution. At some point I would want to reclaim Jesus.

Collateral Damage

"Collateral damage is damage aside from that which was intended."

There are many ways in which collateral damage has been and continues to be caused by many bishops of the Catholic Church as a secondary effect of its treatment of victims. Collateral damage occurs when:

- The Church acts like a sexual offender, reabusing innocent victims in its attempt to avoid more court cases and settlements
- When bishops attempt to silence victims through lies (by applying the doctrine of "mental reservations"), intimidation, or threat of prosecution for court costs
- When bishops protect, defend, and reassign credibly accused and even admitted sexual offenders who cannot be prosecuted due to the statute of limitations
- When bishops refuse to follow the guidelines they themselves have created
- When they do any of these egregious things, they hurt not only the victims, but many, many others.

First of all there are the victims' families, whose trust in the Church and in God is violently assaulted not so much by the original abusive behavior of one sick priest but by the ongoing systematic, legalistic, basically un-Christian behavior of the organization which purports to be led by God's representative and to be Christ's presence in the world.

Then there are our friends, our coworkers, and our therapists. These people all become personally, if indirectly, exposed to the evil perpetrated by Catholic bishops and the Vatican. They all become part of the collateral damage. If they

remain faithful to the Church they will feel a conflict of loyalties, and may find it necessary to cut us out of their lives. If they are family this will cause a fracturing of the family unit. On the other hand, if they are Catholics and remain faithful to us, they may find their support of, and participation in, the Church becomes untenable, and their faith in God questionable. They may, like us, suffer spiritual trauma.

What happens when you destroy someone's hope in a loving God? What happens when you remove someone from their support community, from their rituals of comfort and consolation, renewal and restoration? What happens when you emotionally or physically lock someone out of their spiritual refuge?

What happens is that people can die—from the inside out.

Their soul shrivels; their hope disintegrates; their sense of belonging evaporates. Too often victims fall into an abyss of depression, alcohol and drug abuse, relationship-destruction, self-destruction.

There have been many physical deaths among the community of victims and victims' families, but there are many more spiritual deaths. One aspect of survivor support needs to be a spiritual outreach of some kind. We need to find ways to foster hope, to dialogue about our understanding of God, to share rituals of renewal and enrichment. We need to combat the spiritual death that is part of the collateral damage of the sexual abuse crisis.

What I Have Come to Believe About God and Church

- God isn't Catholic . . . or Muslim or Jewish or Hindu. God is bigger than any single or all combined religions of the world.
- Church rules do not govern my relationship with God; they only affect my relationship to the church community.
- The Catholic Church is a human institution led by human beings, some of whom are exceptionally virtuous, some of whom have made gross mistakes, and some of whom are evil.
- Priests are not God, nor are they Jesus.

- I can meet and know God outside of Catholic Church ritual and doctrine.
- Sex is a gift and can be a holy experience. But it can be misused and become an act of violence. In the same way as all of our gifts, it depends on how we choose to use it.
- Forgiveness of our abusers is possible but very, very difficult, and never excuses their behavior only acknowledges the brokenness that all of us share.

My God-Mother

As part of my healing from sexual abuse by Catholic priests, it has been extremely important to me to find a nonmale image of God. As part of this journey I wrote a story about a little girl called Emm who experienced the love of God as a mother.

> *". . . And sometimes she imagined a God-Mother, serene and kind, with a voice like warm, sugared milk on a cold winter's night—soft and comforting. Wrapped in Mother's gown of twilight blue-gray and bathed with her green eyes, Emm would sleep a gentle sleep. Waking to a bed of leaves, still warm from Her mothering, Emm would never feel alone."*

Catholics tend to fear the feminine when it comes to God, feeling guilty of some kind of paganism if we abandon the Big Daddy in the sky. But feminine images for God are strewn throughout the Bible, both the Old and New Testaments. As far back as St. Augustine, theologians have pointed out that our images of God are always metaphorical, never literal descriptions; God does not have a physical body and therefore has no gender. But with our bishops refusing to make liturgical language or biblical translations gender neutral, my using feminine images for God feels "naughty." It's a good kind of naughty, though, and so affirming for women. *"Our Mother who is in heaven, holy is your name . . ."* It feels so liberating to allow myself a feminine God-image.

83

Recently I have experienced in the United Church of Christ how it is possible to modify scripture translations and prayers to incorporate nongender language for God. Not only is it possible, it is profound and just serves to highlight for me the continued misogyny of the Catholic Church.

Overcoming Grief and Loss Through Self-Parenting

In the summer of 2005 I entered the hospital. The book signings and talks had taken a toll. I was overwhelmed, not sleeping, and finding it hard to be safe. It was a very productive three weeks. I worked hard and learned some important tools for living with PTSD (Post-Traumatic Stress Disorder). That was what I had, apparently. Who knew! Childhood trauma can create post-traumatic stress even years after the event. I had always had symptoms; they hadn't just appeared, but now I was learning how to identify the symptoms and how to survive them. I also began work on my anger.

One of the most marvelous gifts during this hospital stay was a relationship I formed with a teenage girl. A victim of sexual abuse since early childhood, she was embroiled in an ugly legal action against her perpetrator. I wanted to take her home with me and mother her. But I couldn't. And it wouldn't have helped her much, anyway. She would bring her inner demons with her wherever she went until she managed to work through them herself. What's that expression? Wherever you go, there you are!

If you have suffered a loss or a trauma, it goes with you everywhere. It is there in the morning before you are completely awake. It is there when you sober up or come down from whatever form of escapism that your pursue. On bad days you read about it in every newspaper; you find it in every novel and every movie. Even when it is not there, you guess that it is behind the story lurking somewhere ready to jump out, and when it does you say, *"See, I told you. I knew he was a pervert,"* or *"I knew he was going to die."*

My young friend was going to have a very difficult few years ahead of her; I knew that she might not survive. She had courage; she had already come forward and was bringing her perpetrator to justice, but she was losing her family because of the lawsuit. Now she was legally on her own, just turning eighteen, and she already had a tendency towards promiscuity. I wanted to help so badly.

After three weeks I was on "partial" and going home at night. One night I had an inspiration for a story. It was about a teenage girl who doesn't want to grow up and take care of herself and feels life is not fair. I even illustrated it. I gave it to her the day she left. I have no idea how she is doing. I hope she is okay and I hope the gift of the "Fairly-Good Mother" makes her smile sometimes.

It is tempting to succumb to emotional paralysis when you have experienced trauma or loss –relying on other people to care for you and care about you, wanting to be treated like an invalid. I'm not saying we don't deserve some intense TLC and as much time as we need to get ourselves off the sofa and back into life again. I'm just saying that at some point it can become self-indulgent, even self-harming. We can get into the habit of making excuses for ourselves about why we can't do the dishes, take a shower, answer the phone. *"I'm in pain, damn it. Leave me the hell alone." "You don't know what it's like."*

At some point, probably before we feel ready, we have to take a step, and then another. And we have to learn to give ourselves the comfort and support that we have been drawing from others. We have to reach into our own inner resources and "mother" ourselves. And that is what my young friend would need to do if she was going to survive and thrive. What follows is taken from the introduction to the story I wrote for her.

The "Fairly-Good Mother"

If we are very lucky we will have in our lives
women who, though not angels,
are always there for us in our greatest need.

Their wings may be store bought,
and their wands may be duct-taped,
but their hearts are real and they wear them
on the outside of their sometimes very BIG dresses.

Though not necessarily related to us,
they love us truly and always want what is best for us.
And they will tell us what that is
even when we don't want to hear it!

Because they love us,
they refuse to simply say what we want to hear;
because they are only human, they may get it wrong
or say it too strongly.

But we can be sure that what they say and do
is always out of love and concern for us.
They are our "Fairly-Good Mothers."

Talking with Oprah

Have you ever asked yourself which TV show would be the best forum for
your family story? Jerry Springer, CNN nightly news, Oprah? We all have
dialogues going on inside our heads at times, and Oprah is often my internal
muse when I have to work something out and find words for my feelings.

Oprah Winfrey is my internal guru. I talk to her regularly, in the shower
or blow-drying my hair, or driving. And I imagine her responses. They are
always thoughtful and meaningful, not shallow and contrived or manipula-
tive. Oprah seems to want the truth to be told. I've watched her. She expects
sincerity and does not brook duplicity. In our talks she usually just asks me
leading questions, and I find myself thinking more clearly as I formulate an
answer. I learn to be succinct; I become more coherent; my comments become
eloquent. I know that if Oprah believes me (even my imaginary internal companion Oprah) I am believable.

Oprah: Our guest today has had a tragic life. You probably will have
trouble believing her; I did at first. But our initial disbelief didn't upset

or surprise her. You see, Mona didn't fully believe her own life story until all the pieces began to fall into place. Over the past few years, members of her family have reached out to break their silence and own their part in this complex and twisted tale of moral bankruptcy, collusion, rape, abuse, and deception.

The story she tells will shock you, disturb you, perhaps even shake your faith in the Catholic Church, but Mona is adamant that she does not want to hurt people's faith in God. Indeed Mona claims that if it weren't for an ongoing sense of God's presence in her life she might have given up on herself long ago. So please give a warm Oprah welcome to . . .

Ah, Oprah! Maybe one day we will actually meet. But if not, thanks for listening and helping me work through stuff. Thanks for being my imaginary friend. Without knowing it you have helped me examine my thoughts and feelings about the Catholic Church, and you have helped me name the loss. In fact, you have been one of my "Fairly-Good Mothers."

Jesus Was a Victim Too

It may seem self-evident to non-Catholics, but I have come to see the possibility of maintaining a belief in Jesus of Nazareth without supporting the Catholic Church. I wrote the following journal entry during Lent 2006, about the time I decided to leave Catholic education.

Jesus and the Abuse Crisis

I am very angry with my church. I have been angry with my church in different ways since 2002. Sadly, this Easter season I was given new reasons for my anger. Yet this Easter I have also received a gift of grace; I met Jesus again on the road to his cross, and I found in him a victim, too.

87

- Jesus was made an object of public scorn. Catholic victims and their advocates, while championing the rights of children and petitioning for the release of documents that would provide clear evidence of the presence of serial child abusers in the clergy and serial conspirators in the hierarchy, have likewise been made the objects of public scorn.

The comparison continues:
- Jesus spoke up against injustice in his faith community.
- Jesus recognized children, spoke to them, and condemned anyone who would harm a child.
- Jesus was rejected by the leaders of his faith community. He no longer "belonged" because he had dared to speak the Truth and challenge their hypocrisy and immorality.
- Jesus was innocent of a crime but was judged responsible for his arrest and execution because he had incited the crowds by telling the Truth.
- Jesus was mocked, vilified, humiliated, and ultimately abandoned by his community.
- Jesus knew the pain of injustice and abandonment. But unlike many abuse victims, Jesus had a mother and a friend who stayed faithful and continued to believe in him despite what the authorities and community members had accused him of. At least in that way Jesus was blessed. Many sexual abuse victims have lost even these last vestiges of support. But we do not have to carry our crosses on our own.

I believe Jesus would willingly wash the feet of abuse victims, weep over them, and anoint them with oil, in abject sorrow over the sins perpetrated by those exercising authority in his name. I believe that Jesus would willingly take up our crosses and walk in our shoes in an attempt to express his love, in an attempt to convince us that we had not been abandoned. I believe that Jesus already has.

What would Jesus say to the Catholic Church today? What message of hope would he share? There is nothing he could say to defend the indefensible behavior of those Catholic leaders, from local bishops to Vatican officials who have protected and defended abusive priests. I think he would speak to the victims and their families and to the ordinary, faithful and disillusioned Catholics. And more importantly, I think he would listen, and keep listening. Not just for the length of a photo opportunity, not just for fifteen minutes, but for as long as it took to help us with our anger and move us into healing.

I think Jesus would tell us to support each other, to reach out to each other, to share our pain, to create a community of faith, and to continue seeking justice against oppressive and corrupt systems. Jesus would challenge us to really be church/ekklesia—a people gathered with a common purpose and a common faith and commitment to God, Truth, Justice, and to the marginalized. And I think he might remind us that we don't need a certain building or a certain form of religious government to do this.

This Easter season may victims and their advocates continue to rediscover the message and person of Jesus of Nazareth in hopeful and healing ways. And may the voices of truth and reason continue to be heard above the voices of hatred and anger.

Jesus, like God, was not Catholic, and faith in Jesus is not limited to the Catholic Church. Can we have faith in Jesus without Easter Sunday? Certainly. But what about faith in Jesus the Christ?

Personally, I feel that the suffering and death of Jesus have a more profoundly real message than the resurrection of Jesus. The Jesus on the cross teaches us that life isn't fair; sometimes the good do die young; sometimes an innocent person is executed by the state; sometimes the last, best thing anyone can do is stay faithful to their truth and place themselves in God's hands.

Murder, Suicide and God's Plan

Someone posted a letter online with news of the death of a Benedictine monk—his abuser. The death may have brought "closure" for his abuser, he reflected, but not for him. Over the years he had planned then rejected both murder and suicide, but now he expressed sadness—for victims, but also for

his abuser who, he realizes, must have been a troubled and twisted individual. The writer ended the letter with a blessing for his abuser! I was shocked. To have moved from considering murder, not so many years ago, to offering a blessing was incredible, I hesitate to use the word but it seemed—miraculous.

In his words:

"Today I visited Montserrat Abbey, the oldest Benedictine monastery in existence. I went into the Church. I don't know God's plan for me, I don't know God's plan for Fr. Roger, but in my own simple way, I said—And May God bless him."

—C Michael Coode (SNAP Tennessee)

Here was a victim who had retained his faith in God and was now dedicated to advocating for and supporting other victims through the National Survivor Advocates Coalition (NSAC) and through leadership in his local branch of Survivors Network of those Abused by Priests and Religious (SNAP). He had maintained his faith in God despite the overwhelming proof of negligence, deceit, and denial by certain Catholic Bishops. He could still enter a monastery and not run out shaking and crying. He could still pray to a God he believes has a Plan.

I know one thing with absolute certainty: If there is a God and if there is a Plan it doesn't involve abuse of children. What makes most sense to me is that God's plan—call it "the best of all possible worlds"—is thwarted every time someone chooses to reject God in favor of doing evil. And so God has to adjust the plan. My heart tells me that in responding to evil with a blessing Michael has more than lived up to what God would hope for. There is NOTHING more powerful and more loving and healing in the world than responding to evil with goodness, offering a blessing instead of creating more suffering—by hurting oneself or others.

So, I responded to his post and offered Michael a blessing:

May you be blessed and comforted, may the light of Goodness shine upon you and bring you peace, and may you be filled with the healing power of Grace. You are my hero today.

Tender Mercies

Leaving the Catholic Church has hurt, not only because of the betrayal by leaders such as Cardinal George, but also because of the many noble, wise, compassionate, Catholic men and women, teachers, priests, and mentors, whose love and support enabled me to survive since my childhood.

- When home was unsafe, the Church provided a safe harbor.
- When I felt overwhelmed by shame, my priest-confessors reminded me of God's love and grace.
- When I felt abandoned by God, God reached out through the Sisters of La Sainte Union, through the Sisters of Mercy, through Catholic chaplains, through Dominicans, through Jesuits, all of whom took me under their wings at those times when I most needed support.
- When I went looking for answers, the Jesuits trained my mind and prepared me for a career teaching students to think critically and pursue meaning.
- It was to the Church that my youngest brother (my heart when I was a teenager) committed his life and talents.
- It was within the Church that I discovered the man I married.
- It was to the Church that I entrusted my sons' education.
- It was for the Church that I worked for nearly three decades.

Up until 2006 Catholicism had been my religion, my social community, and my spiritual and intellectual home. Leaving the Catholic school system felt like infidelity, because I knew I was also, in my heart, leaving the Church. And what could I do besides teach theology?

Thanks to my months in Houston in 2005 working as an assistant to the Jesuit counseling department, I knew I had office skills. And by the end of

May, 2006, I had taken a job as an Administrative Assistant in a synagogue. No longer working for the Catholic Church gave me the space I needed to truly examine my anger towards the Church and my relationship with God. I have shared those feelings and reflections here.

Working in a Reform synagogue helped me discover a new way of being spiritual and a new community of faithful people. God and I were entering a new phase in our relationship and it was scary, but I was excited and hopeful. Jesus had become a fellow survivor in my eyes, an inspiration and role model. Everything was going to be okay. I could be religious; I could be spiritual. It was all different but it could work. And I had a job and a new community of friends. God was helping me make the transition. I hadn't abandoned God, and God hadn't abandoned me.

Life didn't offer me a long process of recovery from my loss of Catholicism. Less than a year passed after leaving my teaching job and beginning my job in the synagogue before I was faced with a loss that made all the trauma I had ever experienced up until then seem like a rehearsal. Maybe it was by God's grace that I wasn't teaching in a high school when the next crisis happened. It certainly would have been harder for me to grieve with a thousand eyes on me every day, and the loss would have affected my students so much more intensely if I had still been teaching them.

I still believed in God at this point in my life, although my understanding of God continued to evolve. I believed that all of life, and even my particular life, was known to God and was held in the hands of God.

Then one day God let go.

WHEN GOD LETS GO

I felt a loss that sucked the breath out of my entire world.
I lost my hope and I lost my God.

The Story of Malcolm

It was the spring of 2006. Malcolm, my oldest son, was in graduate school, on-site classes having resumed for the first time since Katrina. Mal and I were back home after working in Houston for a whole semester. Being back home was absolutely wonderful, and living with our returnee, graduate school son was also wonderful, probably more so because living with him as an adolescent had been a continuous challenge.

In 2000, when Malcolm left home for college, his dad and I breathed a sigh of relief. Living with Malcolm had been experienced as ongoing tension ever since the onset of adolescence—somewhere around the age of nine, it seemed. Always precocious, Malcolm announced to us at nine that we were "oppressive parents." My husband, an advanced placement, Senior English teacher didn't know whether to congratulate him on his vocabulary or chide him for his attitude. I think we both just laughed.

But it wasn't always so easy to laugh. If my husband had a button, Malcolm had a knack of finding it. It had always been that way. Although they loved each other, they found living with each other sometimes difficult. In many ways it was because they were so alike: the oldest son with the weight of his father's expectations. Both of them intense, anxious, and intelligent. Those same intellectual traits in our second son, James, drove him to try to be first in everything; in Malcolm's case they created anxieties that were sometimes crippling.

We were often torn in our reactions to Malc, laugh or cry, punish or console. And he gave us plenty of opportunities to react. There were the attempts at running away, involving a few hours hiding in some bushes by the neighborhood pumping station. There was his phone call to a boarding school across the lake requesting information about a place at their school. There was the threat of a letter to President Clinton describing the abuse he was receiving from his oppressive parents, abuse like being sent to his room and denied television. And how could we have given him a baby brother? What had he done to deserve such a punishment? In other words, he had a typical first child, older brother life. His greatest burden was probably having to survive being raised by two professional educators. But survive he did. And even thrive. We have to keep reminding ourselves of that fact. We have ribbons and certificates, and photos with beaming smiles, all representing lots of successes and lots of joy, despite his struggles.

From early childhood he loved stories; he wrote his own illustrated version of Hamlet for his first "book" project in third grade, his father having told his sons the story often. He became a voracious reader, swapping books with his teachers by the time he was in seventh grade. In high school he began to write poetry and continued his love of literature. But that didn't mean he was always going to read the books his dad assigned in senior AP English class, at least not until he decided they sounded interesting, and at least once that was after the book quiz! That was typical of Malcolm in his teen years. He loved his dad, and he chose to be in his class, but he was still going to assert his independence.

He wasn't a bookworm, by any means. He read what he wanted when he wanted. And in high school he studied only enough to get by. Master of his own fate and subject to no one and nothing? Not quite. He struggled with bouts of depression and in the ninth grade he had a period of hospitalization, counseling, medications. Then more counseling. More medications. But by now not many of the prescribed pills were ending up inside him. We later found stashes of prescriptions in his room. He hated the side effects of the antidepressants; I can't blame him. I hate them too. So the doctors tried different drugs, different doses. He had hallucinations on one of them. We would all laugh about it eventually, but it was disturbing to witness. He came out of his bedroom into the den and lay on the floor with a plastic shovel telling us he was digging for oil. At sixteen he was four inches taller than his dad and more than fifty pounds heavier. So when he told us he was still taking his medicine, other than force feeding him ourselves, we didn't know what to do. We had to trust that he was.

But Malcolm's childhood and adolescence weren't all depression and confrontation, though. He had wonderful experiences and some very sound mentoring by great role models in the Boy Scouts, and he developed a number of close life-long friends who took the path all the way to Eagle Scout with him. Thanks to his dad, an Eagle Scout himself, both of our sons were enrolled as Tiger Cubs into a great scouting program in our church parish, where they were supported and encouraged to pursue all avenues of leadership. They both made Eagle, and they both deserved it completely.

The scout troop went on weekend camping trips and summer camps every summer. We never withheld scouting events from Malcolm because of report cards or behavior; it was one of the few things that Malcolm loved to do. He eventually became a Boy Scout leader himself and mentored lots of young, troubled scouts. He had a tremendous heart, and somehow the boys who had gotten into trouble with everybody else trusted him. He understood them because he had been like them in some ways. He sometimes stood up to the other adult leaders and insisted that the boys who had misbehaved be given a second chance.

Malcolm graduated from high school in 2000 and received a scholarship to a state honors college with a "Great Books" curriculum that really appealed to him. Lots of philosophy and literature and an emphasis on writing and small group seminars. There were fewer than forty students in his freshman class, so we knew he wouldn't get lost. After starting off as a Computer Science major, he soon realized he belonged in English Literature. It wasn't an

easy decision for him; he hated change. But once he made it everything began to fall into place.

He became fast friends with two of his professors and was trusted by the Dean to be a sitter for her father, a victim of Alzheimer's. There was a rough patch or two along the way, and he felt overwhelmed at the prospect of writing and defending his senior thesis, but he didn't quit. He kept at it, took an extra year and wrote and defended a superb thesis. Mal was there when he defended it, and all three of us saw him graduate. God . . . that was a wonderful day. Malcolm was just beaming. He had such a wonderful, completely encompassing smile. It stretched from the outside corners of his eyes to the widest reaches of his jaw. His hair seemed to smile, too. Long and shaggy, his last stab at rebellion? We didn't care a whit. He could have shaved his head and painted a fleur-de-lis on it; we would still have been proud.

After finishing his degree Malcolm moved back home and enrolled in graduate school. He returned to Troop 491 as an Assistant Scout Master. Then after Katrina, with most of the adult leaders living temporarily in other states, Malcolm assumed the role of Scout Master and kept Troop 491 going. When Malcolm led the advancement ceremony that spring my husband and I sat in the pews bursting with pride. This was our oldest son, the son who had barely made it through speech class in high school because of anxiety. I went through a mental inventory of all the hurdles Malcolm had overcome. I was sure my husband was doing the same thing. And yet here he was, addressing a church full of adults and teenagers on the topic of leadership and doing it with confidence and a smile, despite his nerves.

Having survived Katrina, the three of us were now rebuilding together. Rebuilding each of our schools; rebuilding our Boy Scout Troop. Malcolm was back at graduate school, majoring in English, and planning to teach. We had always known in our hearts that he would make a wonderful teacher. He had the intelligence, the education, the empathy; and now we saw that he had the confidence, too.

We looked at each other through tears; Malcolm was going to make it. Our boy was going to be okay. He was a man now, and in two years time he would be a teacher. We allowed ourselves a private sigh of relief and beamed our smiles at him. Way to go, Malc! Way to go son!

Within a year he had taken his own life.

His death tore a hole in me; I felt a loss that sucked the breath out of my entire world. I lost my hope, and I lost my God. It has taken me more than seven years to get to this place—a place of writing about grief and loss once again. A place where I can step back a little and look at how I survived instead of simply feeling as if I am drowning. After his death, I had to choose to live, and I had to choose it again and again.

Losing Our Son

I have read that losing a child is the most difficult loss anyone can experience. Worse even than the trauma of losing one's spouse. Losing a child to suicide compounds that loss, because added to your grief are intense layers of guilt and anger. Your child has chosen to die rather than live. How could that have happened? How could we not have seen this coming? Who is to blame? But even before the guilt and anger there is the denial: this isn't happening! And a desperate need to turn back the clock just a few hours and fix everything.

It took me six months to be able to write about falling apart after Malcolm's funeral. But I couldn't write about the events of his death until much later. Then I became desperate to write about that day, to record the eulogy, to remember the music at the funeral. I didn't want to forget anything, starting with that last night.

The Night Before

I saw my son the night before—after he came home late from being out with friends. I was lying on the sofa. Was I waiting? He fixed his usual late-night snack to bring to his room.

He didn't put the light on in the kitchen, so from my position lying on the sofa he looked physically shadowed as he stood on the other side of the breakfast bar. He seemed cloudy . . . grey. As if I was looking at him through a fog. Should I have seen a sign in this? I torment myself with that question. It was just the lack of light behind him in the kitchen; there was no message in this, no omen, I tell myself over and over. But looking back, how could I not have known? How could a mother look at her son and not know he was planning to shoot himself in the heart the very next day? How could that much pain not be etched on his face for all the world to see?

I wondered at the time about his mood. But then I wondered every day about his mood. Perhaps if I had wondered aloud to him that night? Perhaps. At least I got to tell him goodnight. His dad was already in bed. He had seen his oldest son, his namesake, for the last time, he just didn't know it yet.

The Day

It was a Monday—March 19th, 2007. Malcolm and I we were both up and about. My husband had already left for work over an hour earlier. He didn't get to see Malcolm that day. Malcolm came through the kitchen, grabbed a section of the newspaper and headed to the bathroom. I called out, Bye, Malc, have a good day, as I left. I remember thinking that I wanted to say, "Love you!" I sometimes did, sometimes didn't. Sensitive to the fact that living back home with one's parents for graduate school was hard enough without a doting mother. Saying I love you was something we all said frequently. Only not that day. Not that day when it would have meant so much to me later to know that I had.

Later, as we pieced together his last day, we learnt that he attended two of his classes at the University of New Orleans and handed in papers in both. But instead of going to his afternoon job on campus he came home picked up two framed photographs that were hanging on the dining-room wall—one of him fishing at Percy Quin, and one of the four of us taken years before—our last formal family portrait. He put the pictures in his backpack. Then he drove to

Lake Pontchartrain, lay down on the levee, and shot himself in the heart. It was 3.30 pm. A Monday.

A neighbor's friend heard the shot and called our neighbor to say she thought someone had just shot himself on the levee near her house, but we didn't hear that story until days after the fact. Some time after 4:30 pm, I don't remember exactly, an unmarked car drove up in front of our house. Two men got out. One was wearing a loud Hawaiian style printed shirt; one was in a coat and tie. That shirt bothered me. That's no way to dress to come to someone's house on serious business, and it looked from their faces like it was serious business. They asked if Malcolm Villarrubia lived here. I said, Father or son? They said, son. When had we seen him last? I didn't know who they were, so I asked them for identification. They went back to their car, and I called my husband to the door. He was at the kitchen sink washing dishes, listening to the news on the radio.

It's the police. Something about Malcolm.

What is it? He asked.

I don't know.

They showed us their identification. Can we come in? We said yes; there didn't seem to be much choice. We couldn't choose not hear what they had to say; we couldn't just go back to the dishes and the computer and wish it away. There was something we had to hear, and both of us felt without speaking that whatever it was, it was really bad. But we had weathered storms with Malcolm before. Whatever it was, we would support him, and we would get through it together. We always had.

We all sat down at the kitchen table. They produced Malcolm's backpack. There were smears of red on it. I couldn't take my eyes of it.

Do you have a recent picture of your son? Is this his wallet?

After several minutes of questions one detective finally said,

There's no easy way of saying this, your son is dead.

Darkness.

Words . . . more words . . .

We found his body . . . shot . . . looks like he took his own life . . .

Words . . . crying . . .

I don't understand.

My husband standing next to me, hugging, sobbing. Then sitting again.

We want to see him.

I'm sorry his body has been taken to the morgue. We will have his body sent to the funeral home. You will be able to see him there.

His body . . . not him. Already a body, not a person.

Here's a phone number. You can call about the autopsy.

What do we do now?

You'll need to make arrangements.

Arrangements?

For the funeral. They should release his body by Wednesday. You can arrange a funeral for Thursday or Friday.

Funeral?

We have to arrange a funeral. For our son. We have to bury our son. How do we do that?

Call this number at the funeral home; they will help you with all the arrangements.

Arrangements. Such a clinical word.

Thank you.

We're sorry for your loss.

They really say that. Sorry for your loss. Loss. We have lost our son. Can't we find him again?

When is Malcolm coming home? He should be home by now. I don't understand.

They left. We had to make calls. First Tommy and Sharon, the closest family members, just around the block. They would help us take the next few steps. What are the next few steps? Calls. We have to call our son, James, Malcolm's brother. Oh God. How to tell him? But we have to tell him. Word will spread fast. We looked up the University of Virginia phone numbers on the website, called James' dean of students, phoned one of his friends to ask

him to go over and make sure he was not alone when we talked to him. Then we phoned James. He would get someone to fly home with him from Virginia. Good. Good.

Family started arriving. Talking, crying, hugging. Friends started arriving. My boss from work. But I was gone by then. Walking to the levee. They had been talking about Malcolm in the past tense. I couldn't bear it. Don't bury him so quickly. He isn't cold yet. He could still come home and tell us it was a mistake. He didn't mean to do it. The night isn't over yet. Let me go to the lake where he died, maybe I can find him. Maybe he is just lost. I walked for blocks in bare feet. Didn't notice until the shells on the levee. Sat on the top of the levee in the dark, looking out at the lake. Darkness.

Is this where he died?

There had been a note in his bag for us. It had a smudge of blood on it, as if the police had tried to wipe it clean.

"It's not your fault, it was never your fault . . . I will be where the water meets the shore."

A poet even in death. Trying to take care of us with a promise to be at the water's edge. But he wasn't there. I looked and looked. I walked up and down the levee. He wasn't there. He lied.

Voices calling out to me, but I didn't hear them. People had gone looking, taking another path to the lake. I didn't see them. It was dark. Later I walked home. Not aware yet of the ant bites on my feet. I would feel that pain later, when all the pain became real.

Our Final Farewell

I want to share Malcolm's eulogy because it will help you to know my son. And I want you to know my son. Mal, James, and I wrote the eulogy together and read it at the funeral together, bonded by our grief and our desire that Malcolm's story be told and heard and Malcolm's life be honored, even in the face of his tragic death.

The Eulogy

MAL

I am Malcolm's dad, and I stand here together with Mona, Malcolm's mom, and with James, Malcolm's brother. Today we have the unenviable duties of celebrating Malcolm's life and then saying goodbye.

Let me first thank all of you who are here today out of love and support for Malcolm and for us. We know that there are friends here today from Jesuit, Dominican, UNO, Tulane, St. Clement of Rome Parish, Touro Synagogue, the men and boys of Troop 491 and from as far way as Liverpool, England. You presence and your kindness and prayers have sustained us. We are humbled. In speaking to so many of you, in reading the text messages Malcolm is still receiving, and in seeing the many postings on Facebook, we have learned—even more than we knew before—how widely and deeply Malcolm was loved.

Of course, we have loved him deeply for 24 years. Therefore in the past few days all of us have asked over and over again, why? Why would Malcolm, so tender-hearted and sensitive and gifted and so deeply loved, why would he be, in the end, so terrified of life?

Those of us who knew Malc well know that if he were here, he would jump in right now to lighten the moment for us. Proudly sporting his South Park tie, he would either quote Homer Simpson or utter one of his wonderful Malcolmisms. Then he would say, Dad, enough with the philosophizing. Just tell a story.

And he would be right. Whether we are comfortable with it or not, we are left with the mysteriousness of life. The answers we are looking for are ultimately known only by our good Lord. Malcolm was a wonderful and precious gift from God to Mona and me and James, and to all of us. He will always be a gift.

MONA

So, here are a few stories that celebrate who and what Malc was:

1) When Malcolm was very small he found a live crawfish making its way down the sidewalk in front of our house—an escapee from a neighbor's crawfish boil. Rather than return the crawfish to its imminent death, he insisted that I drive him and the crawfish six blocks to the local canal. He wanted life for that crawfish. Soon after that he brought home his first pet: Harriet the hermit crab rescued from the beach at Biloxi. Graduating from crustaceans, he then rescued turtles. He had Browny 1, Browny 2, and then . . . Greeny. Malcolm had a unique and spare way with words. As a small child his favorite soft toy was called, simply, "Friend."

2) There was nothing Malcolm looked forward to more than our week-long family vacation at Percy Quin state park each summer. His absolute greatest joy was being at dawn or dusk waist deep in the lake, walking the shore, whipping his fly rod—in touch with the quiet life of the water and trees and fish—and an occasional alligator. It was at Percy Quin, in the cramped sleeping arrangements, at the exciting meals, and in the long after-dinner conversations, that he learned family history, and the love of his grandparents, Shirley and Mac, and felt the love of his uncles, Tom and David and Pete, and their beautiful families. Fishing and family. Malcolm loved Percy Quin.

3) Malc carried his love of nature and fishing into his Jesuit Service Project—serving as a camp counselor for children with muscular dystrophy. What began as a required service project, he continued for 4 more years as an act of love. Malcolm had a fierce desire to make a positive difference in kids' lives. He helped a boy in an electric wheel chair land his first fish by hooking a line with bunny bread and tying it to the boy's wheelchair. What had seemed impossible for that child, Malcolm made possible. It would have been hard to tell who was more proud of that fish.

MAL

4) After Katrina, Mona and I stayed four months in Houston, committed to teaching our displaced Jesuit boys at Strake Jesuit. Malcolm returned as quickly as he could to our home in Metairie. For those four months he was the man of our house. Heroically, he lived alone, cleaned debris, patched our roof, fought fridge funk, and ate army rations for nearly a month. Malcolm persevered. He reveled in surviving the trying conditions.

As numbers slowly trickled back to Metairie, a call went out for a Scoutmaster for Troop 491, the troop Malc had long been a member of. As an Eagle Scout himself, he knew the importance of once again giving these young men adventure and joy and normalcy. Malcolm stepped forward, a 23 year old young man, and was Scoutmaster for a year. He was beloved by his scouts.

In these last two years, while Malcolm lived at home with Mona and me—and attended graduate school at UNO, Malcolm has been a joy to live with. He was a wonderful son. And James is a wonderful son. There has never been a single minute when Mona and I have not been proud of our two boys—both outstanding young men. Malcolm was always quick to hug us and tell us over and over again that he loved us. But more than a loving son, Malc had become a good friend to us. We talked about literature and God and Jesus and life. We ate sushi, watched movies, shared stories, and laughed. We are a family of such deep love for each other.

But the truth is that there are also darker stories, stories of past depression. Malcolm questioned and probed life and god at every turn. As much as there was about life that gave him joy, there were things that upset him. He worried about so many people. Sensitive and tender, he was quick to carry others' burdens, but sadly, in the end, he could not bear his own.

For years Mona and I did everything we could to nurture him out of his fears. He really seemed to have risen above his depression. In these

last two years at home with us he seemed the happiest he has ever been. Many of you have said the same. Sadly, we now know there was a truth he hid too deep for any of us to fathom. Knowing Malc, he fought his horrors alone because he did not want to burden the very people whom he loved and knew loved him.

There are 1000s of other stories. His incredible wit and intellect, his joy in verbal sparring, pushing propositions to their most absurd conclusions and doing so with a straight face—until he cracked a broad smile and you knew that he was just messing with your head.

JAMES

I'm going to try to explain a little about Malcolm as a friend and as a brother. I've talked to his friends and searched through stories. I've tried to gather a few Malcomisms that we can remember him by. For example,

He would make little raps when the conversation lulled.

He would say "Gerb" or "Gerbil" a lot.

He would say "I got that cupcake wodie."

He would say "Gobble Gobble" a lot.

He would quote Neverending Story a lot.

Most of all "Snert," "Blergen."

Beyond the Malcolmisms, I've also tried to think of what Malcolm would want said here. What he would like us to walk away with.

First, learn how to fish. It brought him so much happiness, I'm sure we can find some in it too.

Second, Share what you know with kids. Brighten their days. Give them the courage to push forward, to weather the storms. Teach them to be responsible men and women. Most of all, listen to them—they will make you smile when you least expect it. Some people think Malcolm would've been a great father or uncle. Well, forget that—he WAS a great father for so many kids in so many ways.

Third, if you ever miss him or someone else—write them a letter. Just get it all down on paper. Then you can rest for a bit. It was one of the first things he ever told his friend Sean to do—and they've been friends ever since. Must have been good advice.

Fourth, listen to Johnny Cash, the Empire of the Sun soundtrack, and Tool. I think you'll understand him a bit more that way.

Fifth, find the stupidity, the irony, and mostly the hilarity of life. If Malcolm was good at anything it was that. He could take a drab, dark, philosophical topic and cut it straight to the core. He could summarize the whole thing in one phrase—AND make it funny. You have to be of a certain brilliance to do what he did.

Finally, he would say "PERSPECTIVE IS EVERYTHING." He knew there was happiness in the world. He tried in so many ways to change his perspective, to find that happiness and to enjoy it. Call it the downside of brilliance or just bad body chemistry, whatever it was . . . he struggled for so long to find that happiness. We owe it to him to find it, to be joyful every day.

Personally, I will miss waking up Christmas morning and talking about what was in our stockings. I will miss "Big Tackle" with dad. I will miss carpet soccer in the den. I will miss his music and his bass system—waking up the neighborhood. I will miss his insane humor and his unique perspective on life. I will miss my brother.

But if you ever want to hang out with him, you still can. Find a place—where the water meets the shore. He'll be there, probably fishing, and willing to listen to everything you have to say. Like a good friend, like a good brother.

MAL

What more in these final moments can I say about my wonderful son who shared my name and who made me proud every day? These stories show us he was immensely caring, tender-hearted, generous, a loving son and brother, and a faithful friend to so many.

Malcolm had learned well the core lesson of Jesuit High School and of Jesus, to be a Man for Others. He was so much a man for others. Sadly, however, what he could so generously and happily give to others, he could not find a way to give to himself—love.

To Malcolm, who now lies in his casket, I say again, I love you. Mom and James love you. God loves you. All of us love you. We wish you had found a way to love yourself as much as all of us here today love you.

I don't want to end these moments with our words but with some of Malc's. He was a very fine poet. I want to read a short poem he wrote about his happiest times—fishing with his uncles at Percy Quinn.

Early Risers
There were only four up at this hour,
me, Uncle Dave, Uncle Pete, and the sun
(and the sun was running late).
Waste deep and entwined in fly line
I watched
their ancient motor shove the rented skiff
to the far side, where the big ones roam,
or so the theory goes.
When the air got thick they turned back toward
Smoked bacon and cheese grits
with only jokes and grime to show
and we sipped chicory coffee black.
I laughed with Dad and his brothers about
ant piles, and stocks, and family,
while quietly we all thought about
the ones that get away.

*   *   *

Fragments

It was impossible to reflect on what I was feeling for those first few months. It was all I could do to simply be in the feelings and to breathe. Then slowly I began to write again. First it was just pieces. Pieces I wanted, needed, to remember.

Heartbreak . . .

is when all the air leaves the room because you hear the words, ". . . we found your son's body . . ." and you don't hear anything else. But someone in the background is screaming, "I don't understand, I don't understand . . ." and it might be you.

The last kiss . . .

A few days before he died. He was at the computer in the den. He needed to use our printer. I walked up behind him and bent down and kissed the top of his head. I remember it still. His smell, his scratchy, thick hair. He had his granddad Hayes' hair. The next time I kissed him was the day we saw his body. His skin was cold but his hair felt the same. He was dressed in his good shirt and his South Park tie. The funeral parlor staff had brushed his hair back, so I had to pull it forward and muss it a bit so it would look more natural. That was the last kiss, but it didn't count, he couldn't feel it any more.

Breaking . . .

It was a Friday when we buried Malcolm. The next day I broke into pieces. Like a mirror made of ice, the pieces of me melted and I evaporated. I looked in the mirror, and I wasn't there; I think I just couldn't be present to the hurt. I took a razor to my arm and cut, "I love you Malc, be at peace." I wanted it to last forever. I didn't feel the pain. The blood surprised me; I felt like a spectator.

Becoming Angry at God

The pain, the shock, the emptiness . . . they were overwhelming. I was drowning in my feelings and frequently felt barely able to function. Where

was my faith? The faith that had carried me through my childhood and adolescence, through my disillusionment with the Church, the faith in a God who held me when all around me was chaos, that faith deserted me. God deserted me. At least that was how it felt. And I became angry at God.

I was a mother who had lost her child and wondered if she had been fooled all her life, who wondered if there really was a God after all, and who wanted to know where she could direct all her anger if the universe was, after all, just one great big cosmic joke with no punchline.

Mother Teresa spent most of her adult life in a spiritual darkness, no longer feeling the presence of God, struggling with an emptiness, a resounding silence. Now I knew that silence. I had expected to feel God's presence, to sense the hand of God holding me. I had felt it many times in my life. I had sensed a presence under the safety and immensity of the night sky, and in my heart. I had felt transported when singing in Church, or when listening to the symphony. Such music could convince me there was a God. I had known it in every cell of my being; such beauty could not come from nothing, be for nothing.

These experiences of momentary transcendence had kept my faith alive, kept me committed to teaching religion, kept me hopeful, optimistic and centered. When I was depressed, it was often sacred music that had the power to lift me out of my fear, out from under the burden of my past. Music had the power to touch my soul and help me heal. When I sang "I Can Only Imagine" or "O Magnum Mysterium," or when I heard the second movement of Beethoven's Seventh Symphony, or Samuel Barber's "Adagio for Strings," I knew, I just knew, that God had a part in its creation. This sublime beauty was not the result of chaos and chance and random astrophysical events. It couldn't be. And the night sky always held such mystery and magnificence. Somehow it was as if I was looking at God's blueprints for life.

We lived in a neighborhood near Lake Pontchartrain, and I would walk or ride my bike there in the evening and watch the sun set. Malcolm loved the lake, too. It was one of many things we shared, although he focused more on fishing than star gazing. After he was gone, I was glad they were doing construction on the levees, because that meant I couldn't walk there, and it wasn't safe for me to walk there anymore. I wasn't safe with my thoughts.

After Malcolm was gone. The words seem so casual, so natural. But there was nothing casual or natural about the way he left us. And now there was no beauty to be found, and if there was a God, God seemed to have become the Cosmic Sadist of C.S. Lewis's greatest fears. Why else would God have let my son die without giving me a warning, without helping me to save him? There was no redeeming value in Malcolm's death, just pain and loss. How could a loving God have allowed this to happen?

Hummingbird

Written six months after Malcolm's death.

Born and raised Catholic, a religious educator for 27 years, I find that it hurts to believe in God right now. In self-defense I have discovered the comfort of agnosticism. The maybe; the hope. My son's last writings, before he took his own life at the age of 24, speak of a hope that somehow all that he loved in life, those people and places most precious to him, were not lost to him forever. And that is all I have to cling to right now. I try to pray, but I have no idea to what or to whom I am praying. I struggle with "nouning" it let alone naming "It." So I talk to my son. I talk to the sky. I talk to myself. I even imagine talking to Oprah Winfrey again, as if somehow being on her show would immediately make me eloquent, help me put into words what I can't even manage to think.

Unfortunately for me there have been many well-intentioned people all too willing to put my feelings and my faith into words for me. God is with you, I am told. Look for a sign; there will be signs everywhere. In pennies on the ground, in butterflies. A sign that your son is at peace. A sign that your son is with you, that everything is okay. But everything is not okay. Some kind of sign from God before my son succumbed to a despair we didn't even guess at—that would have been useful. That would have been evidence of an "All

111

Powerful" who gives a damn. But not butterflies, not pennies, and certainly not now. Now all I want to do is wail and sob.

The morning after my son's funeral I was overcome by a need to talk to him, to touch him. The closest I could come to his own body was the body through which he entered the world—my own. Words on paper did not suffice. This unbearable and unimaginable pain required a totally different canvas. My arm became that canvas, and I wrote my goodbye note with a razor, "I love you Malc, be at peace." It felt like the sanest thing I had done all week. Much more rational than planning readings and songs he would never hear or buying new underwear he would never feel against his skin. I had made it through those responsibilities; I had co-written his eulogy and taken part in its reading. I had greeted and hugged hundreds of his friends. But it all felt unreal. Kissing his head and ruffling his hair felt real, but then they closed the coffin, and I couldn't touch him or kiss him ever again. The next morning, as I cut my arm, I felt him somehow still part of me, that ontological connection of mother and child, and I knew he would read my note.

Earlier that morning as I lay awake in the after-fog of a sleeping pill, I saw or hallucinated a hummingbird hovering in the doorway of my bathroom. A sign? I stumbled to the computer to look up the mythological symbolism of hummingbirds. But after a few minutes I realized how ridiculous I was being. If Malcolm had wanted to give me a sign it would not have been a humming-bird, it would have been a blue jay, maybe. But you know what would have been a real sign, hearing him fart. A good, deep reverberating one. That would be a sign that all is well with my son. It would call to mind the mornings when he would fart, crack a smile from ear to ear, grab the newspaper and make some comment about bodily functions to come and reading matter required. Gross, real, earthy, beautiful . . . my son. The king of dead baby jokes and the author of a compendium of bathroom musings and collected quotes such as, *"What if the Hokey Pokey really is what it's all about?"*

Despite my doubt that it was a sign of some kind, I nonetheless did some reading about hummingbirds. Why would my brain throw out the image of a hummingbird, I wondered? I was interested to learn that because of its speed, the hummingbird is known as a messenger and stopper of time. The hummingbird is able to fly backwards, suggesting to some interpreters that we can look back on our past but that we must not dwell on our past; we need to move forward. In the Andes of South America the hummingbird is a symbol of resurrection. It seems to die on cold nights, but comes back to life again at sunrise. The hummingbird is also interpreted as a symbol of love, joy, and beauty. When we observe the hummingbird hovering over flowers while drinking nectar, we are reminded to savor each moment, and appreciate the things we love.

Maybe somewhere in my head I had stored this information about hummingbirds, and that was why I saw one. I don't know. Maybe it was a sign after all. Whatever it was, it was beautiful to wake up to.

Too Soon

Journal entry—September, 2007

I miss the smell of my son. The smoky campfire smell after a scout trip, the rankness of sweat and bait after an evening's fishing at the lake. I just miss the smell of him. And no butterfly, or hummingbird, however beautiful, will ever be able to recall him to my senses. Maybe a dead fish, but not a bird.

The first fight my husband and I had after our son's death was over the fact that he washed the bedding from Malcolm's bed. But we've closed the bedroom door again; we had done too much. It wasn't time.

I have created a little "prayer shelf" with a religious icon, my son's photo, some incense, a candle, and a prayer card. It grew slowly; there was no purposeful imitation of any religious tradition, it just feels right. Sometimes I talk to him, sometimes I read the prayer card. Always, I cry. I don't feel close to any Higher Power, I just feel absolute and unalterable loss.

Last week I visited my son's grave for the first time. It had been six months, but even so I was not ready. I don't know what will ever make me ready. I lose my breath every time I think of him alone in the earth. The

days since then have felt much like the first month after his death, the pain coming in waves.

But I'm trying to think more positively. I am forcing myself to smile more. I even danced last Saturday. And I am trying to focus on my son as a gift. But then I come back to the question, To what or to whom do I give thanks? And I realize that I miss my faith. Right now, like my son, all I have is hope.

Living in the Loss

Journal entry—April 3, 2008

We experience all kinds of loss every day. Petty losses like the loss of an argument or the temporary loss of the TV remote control. Then there are the more significant losses. Loss of friends and family who move to other cities. Loss of peace of mind that results from excessive anxiety and stress. Loss of leisure time when we take on the extra responsibilities of parenthood, or elder care, or a promotion at work. And, finally, there are the profound losses: the end of a relationship, the permanent loss of good health, the death of a loved one. I know that my loss is not unique, not even unusual, but that doesn't make it any easier.

In the past I always had room for God in my heart and in my life. But, for a year now, grief has smothered my gratitude. From the very beginning I looked at my son's life as a gift from God. I was sick during most of my pregnancy and lost his twin, but Malcolm survived. They say that twins often exhibit an uncanny connection, so perhaps he felt a loss growing up that he couldn't explain, a part of himself that was missing. I'm sure it was hard for him to know his life came with a death. Growing up, when he got frustrated and angry, he would say, I didn't ask to be born. Maybe he felt that he had to make up for his twin's death, that he had to somehow be worthy enough for two lives in order to deserve to be alive himself. Feeling worthy was a life-long struggle for him, a battle he ultimately lost.

I was able to love my son for 24 years, to hold his hand, drive him to school, make him supper, patch his uniform, scratch his back, hug and kiss him goodnight, send him off to high school and eventually college. After college there was graduate school and moving back home. Oh, the dread of living with a teenage rebel again. But he was a man, now. He loved and appreciated his life with us, and told us so on many occasions. We laughed together at memories of his teenage exploits. He seemed to have settled into himself. But looking back I have to wonder if he ever really heard any of the praise or approval people expressed during his last few years.

I may be grateful for my years with my son, even the difficult years, but they weren't enough. Each night it is possible to imagine him alive and escape into dreams where I relive family memories. But each morning I awake to the awareness of loss all over again. The shock isn't as great as it was that first day after his death, but somehow the loss is always a surprise, a jolt to my senses followed by an overwhelming heaviness. Breathing requires a conscious effort as I sit on the edge of the bed and wait for the panic to subside enough to let me begin my day. I survived yesterday, I can make it through today, I tell myself, only partly believing it. Somehow surviving seems a betrayal. The fact that life goes on seems almost grotesque. Some kind of existential joke.

These last couple of months, I have felt angry with myself for my self-pity, for writing self-indulgent reflections. Perhaps it is easier to be angry at myself than God. I know it is impossible to be angry at my son. It would feel like the ultimate betrayal. But how can I support his act of self-annihilation? I can't. Not out of some religious righteousness, but out of anger over the vastness of the loss. I didn't lose my son on my own; the loss is shared by his father and brother, his cousins, aunts and uncles, his close friends, even those who were not so close but knew him and appreciated his humor, compassion and kindness. At his funeral hundreds lined up to say goodbye. We stood for three hours as people we knew, and people we had never met, told us how much Malcolm had touched their lives.

Perhaps I am beginning to be angry at him. How could he hurt so many people? But the truth is I don't think he imagined for a second that his death would cause so much pain to so many. I don't think he was able to internalize

the love people expressed to him; in fact I don't know that he even recognized it as love. That would require that he felt he deserved to be loved, and I don't think he ever did.

Just yesterday a young man whom my son had mentored through a difficult adolescence stopped me on the street to give me a hug. He shared with me how difficult his year had been; my son's death had broken him, he said. His pain was palpable; his love as apparent as the tremble at the corner of his mouth. I felt helpless, unable to offer consolation. Loss speaking to loss. Hearts too full and too empty.

Psychology teaches that the experience of loss will be compounded when there is a history of loss. So, what does this mean for me and for all those grieving the loss of my son? Living as we do in a post-Katrina New Orleans, we all have multiple losses to contend with, so our feelings of loss are magnified. But new buildings are going up, and houses are being reclaimed. The blighted neighborhoods are slowly healing, the debris being swept away. It has been nearly three years since the storm, and signs of renewal are overtaking signs of chaos and decay. But it has only been a year since my son's suicide, so we are still experiencing the effects of that storm. Emotional debris still dominates our landscape.

This has been a year of firsts: first Father's Day, first Christmas, first anniversary of my son's death. So many firsts. They say the second year is easier, but in some ways I am not ready for it to be easier. I need to live in the loss a while longer.

Carrying On

Journal entry—May 1, 2008

They say our greatest gifts are also our greatest burdens. My son's gifts included compassion and empathy, and as a result many people turned to him for support—teens, college peers, even the parents of teens. He carried a lot of pain, his own and others.

Did my abuse help to darken the world in which Malcolm found himself? No doubt. I realize that it was not the reason for his death, but it must have made living a greater struggle for him. Did he dread a future filled with the same kind of ongoing battle with depression he witnessed in my life? Did he feel unable to share his struggle for fear that he would be adding to my own? Did he fear having to carry me?

I am so sorry, Malc, for adding to your pain. I wish I had another chance to carry you and ease your suffering. I love you so much.

My son carried his pain for as long as he could. He can't carry it anymore, but maybe I can, at least a small part of it. And that is how I can love my son. I can be there for his friends and for the rest of our family. I can keep going and choose not to add to the pain. That in itself takes a commitment.

There is a song I used to sing that has these words, "Lay down your burden, I will carry you, I will carry you my child." I can no longer carry my son in my arms, but I can still carry him in my heart.

There is Nothing Poetic or Romantic About Suicide
Journal entry—June 27, 2008

Mourning a loss is not a poetic or romantic experience the way it is portrayed in old movies when the heroine lies back on her soft pillows in her silk gown and weeps gently while the hero kneels by her side delicately holding her hand. In real life there is no accompanying sound track, and there is a lot more emotional mess. Screaming at an empty room, sobbing over an empty chair. Lots of red, swollen eyes, running noses and balled up tissues. Lots of unwashed hair and socks. There is no one holding your hand, because anyone close to you is trying desperately to hold themselves together. There are piles of unwashed dishes and clothes, and food going moldy in the fridge. For weeks and months these things are not important. We manage to shower and go to work and function there, and then we come home and we lose all our strength . . . we just pour ourselves into a chair or onto the sofa and pray for sleep. We have gotten better about eating together again.

But the system breaks down on the weekends when I might wear my pajamas for 36 hours straight and lie on the sofa crying at movies; when my husband weeps and fusses to himself and to his son as he mows the grass; when neither of us has the energy to shower or cook or shop or do any of those normal things we do when we have to get up for work.

It's not easy to be around the mother of a suicide. I know that. I understand the reluctance of many friends to reach out, and this makes me even more grateful for the ones who do. I was especially grateful when friends asked about my son and his death and how I was doing, knowing that I might actually tell them and they wouldn't be able to leave for a while. Now, after a year, I am grateful when cousins bring his name into conversations and stories are shared. And I am grateful when people remember his anniversary and his birthday.

Right now I am physically run down and developing minor health issues, recurrent sinus infections, boils and rashes. I need to sleep better and eat more healthfully and avoid stress. I know . . . that's a joke! Right? But we are taking three days over July 4th weekend to go to the coast. And I love being by the sea. I long just to sit and stare and watch the sunset, and remember good times with our two boys playing sandcastles and going island hopping on the sand bars at low tide at night, carrying flashlights and chasing sand crabs.

I remember all of us sharing one bedroom in the vacation apartment and being able to watch my boys competing for space even in their sleep. I remember as the years passed wondering if they were too old for me to kiss them on their cheeks at bedtime and waiting 'til they slept instead. I remember watching them play in the pool with their dad. Big tackle. Big, big smiles. I wonder whatever happened to Malcolm's joy.

Is Joy Possible?

Journal entry—June 2, 2008

Why is it we expect life to be good? Statistically speaking this planet should not even have life on it; the fact that we exist at all defies the laws of probability.

But here we are. And we aren't just here, we are aware that we are here. We don't just live and die, we think, choose, create, love. Life is difficult, full of sorrow and struggle. But maybe that is the norm. What is amazing is that there is so much more. Each day it is possible to be surprised by joy . . . apologies to C.S. Lewis for borrowing his book title. So perhaps we should not look at suffering as evidence that God doesn't exist, but look at joy as evidence that God does.

Journal entry—July 25, 2008

Being happy can make me feel guilty, as if I have forgotten to be sad about my son's death, as if I have forgotten him. That would be impossible, of course. But you can't feel the intensity of the loss all the time. It is crushing. Luckily our minds won't allow us to; eventually we begin to feel other things besides pain, despite ourselves. And of course it is okay to feel happy. Nothing is ever just one layer, emotionally speaking.

We recently spent a few days at The Balmoral Inn in Biloxi, a place we spent many a summer vacation with our boys. Lots of good memories. Precious memories of our boys. Life was good. And now it is good and bad at the same time.

I don't know how to do this mourning thing and still enjoy life; there is no right way. It seems it is possible to experience joy and still be experiencing loss. What is good is that thinking about my son being "with me" rather than "gone" has helped. I will just have to learn to live with emotional layers and not deprive myself of joy out of a sense of guilt. I know my son would want me to find some joy again.

Life Goes on; Death Goes on
Journal entry—October 14, 2008

When your child dies it feels as if the world should end, that nothing could possibly go on as normal. But the world absorbs the death of your child and

keeps on going, seemingly indifferent. The continuation of mundane existence seems to highlight the horror of your loss.

How can I be making small talk? How can I be worrying about what to wear, what to eat? Yet I do. The world goes on and I with it, even though it feels like a betrayal of my son.

And not only life goes on, but death, too. People don't stop living and people don't stop dying. You think you can't possibly feel any more pain than you have already felt, and then someone you care about dies, and you realize that your capacity for pain just grows to accommodate each successive tragedy.

On Saturday we buried a friend. We gathered to mark his passing and honor his life. For a few hours the world seemed to hold its breath and we grieved together. Then we turned away from each other and returned to the ordinary and mundane. But the world to which we returned was a world changed, a world a little less bright, a little less loving, because he was no longer there.

All will be well, according to Julian of Norwich. Do I believe that? I don't know what I believe any more, but my friend believed. And wherever he is, he is no longer in pain, and for that I am grateful. Could we have loved him more? Yes. Could we have saved him? No. I lived with my son Malcolm; I saw him every day and ate with him most evenings. We talked. We went out for lunch. We shared jokes and books and ideas. But I didn't know that he was planning to take his life. And even if I had, I'm not sure what I could have done other than have him committed for a while. But then what? He was 24, an adult. I couldn't baby sit him anymore.

It is arrogant of us to think we can save another human being. We can't—unless they want to be saved. All we can do is try to save ourselves and try to love each other a little more.

The Face of Suicide

Journal entry—October 20, 2008

We looked through boxes of photos tonight. It was wonderful to see Malcolm smiling and remind ourselves that he was happy and he was loved and he had some great times. My husband had commented the other day, *Did Malcolm ever smile like that?* on seeing a toddler beaming with pure joy. And the answer is, *Yes, of course he did.* And thankfully we have lots of photos to prove it to ourselves whenever we doubt it again.

A child is never just happy or just sad; life is never just easy or just difficult. And it is trite to say it will get better, because I am not sure it will. But it will get bearable, I hope. There will be more happiness and there will be more sadness. That's just the way it is.

Journal entry—December 6, 2009

The family walked in the first New Orleans *Out of Darkness* AFSP (American Foundation for Suicide Prevention) fundraiser yesterday. It was a very moving experience because so many of my husband's extended family came out to walk with us. And it was in the 40s with a wind chill in the 30s, which are arctic conditions for New Orleans. I wore a T-shirt with Malcolm's picture on . . . showing his wonderful smile. People need to know what the face of suicide looks like—it can look like the life of the party! Of course all of us there knew that already, but maybe you didn't.

Do we ever really know what is going on inside another person? He may seem completely "together" but actually be falling apart. She doesn't seem to need encouragement but might be suffering in a private darkness and needing desperately to experience a little piece of hope. We may never know it, but a single, small, unexpected act of kindness towards another person may mean the difference between hope and despair, between life and death.

Seeing Visions; Dreaming Dreams
Journal entry—January 19, 2009

Driving last week I saw a young man in a car one lane over. His hands rested on the wheel. All of a sudden they were Malcolm's hands. Not looking like but looking as if they were really his. I know I wasn't really seeing Malcolm;

my mind was playing tricks on me, filling in an image it recalled from my memory. But rational thinking played no part in the experience.

As I watch, I suddenly can't breathe, and there's a lump in my throat. I want to follow the car and keep seeing Malcolm's hands on the wheel, but the car pulls off and turns. I'm stuck in my lane. I begin crying.

Today, driving down my street I saw a red Honda coming towards me, a car like Malcolm's. And as it passed me, I saw him behind the wheel.

As I write this my throat clenches up one more time. I hope I see him again soon; I don't care that it isn't real. An embodied memory is better than nothing. This nothing is so permanent.

Isn't it Time to Move On?

Journal entry—March 24, 2009

"Thousands of mothers lose a child every day." "Everybody has a cross to bear." "Think about your other son."

These are a few of the "reasonable" but insensitive responses people might be thinking even if they do not share them. I even say the same things to myself, sometimes. But Malcolm was my son. Bone of my bone, flesh of my flesh, as Genesis Chapter 2 describes the creation of the woman from the man. Although the end of this story in Genesis is used as a metaphor for marriage, man and woman joining again as one flesh, the language of bone from bone and flesh from flesh is much better suited to parenthood, especially mother-hood. A child is literally part of a mother's body, fed by her blood. Losing a child is like losing a limb. The scar is permanent and the pain continues long after the loss, like the pain suffered by an amputee in a leg that is no longer part of her body.

So to anyone who dares wonder if it is time for me to get over my grief I say, Have your leg amputated and in two years I will ask you if you are ready to move on from your loss. Then we can talk.

Time . . .

doesn't need our permission,

draws the color out of our memories,

numbs our pain,

unleashes it full force

and then erodes it—the final injury,

passes us by

spectators in our own lives,

the movie screen

with lips out of sync with sound

who is that?

she looks familiar

it is me.

We Are All of Us Broken

Journal entry—March 28, 2009

We are all broken to some degree. You can't reach mid-life without being touched by tragedy or loss, and often not even one's teens. So what holds you together within yourself? Each of us has to find something! Sadly, it is sometimes self-harming things like abusing drugs, food or alcohol, or obsessing over work, money or possessions.

And what bonds you to others?

In the Villarrubia family we have a saying, originating with the oldest grandchild, *Don't mess with the glue!* For us, family is the glue that holds us together. And much of that glue owes its binding power to one week we share in a Mississippi state park at the end of July—the stickiest part of a southern summer. I often reference this experience in my writing because it was so important to Malcolm.

When we gather for family events or holidays all you have to say is, the bat cabin, gloop, skit night, or Intermission and vivid, riotous collective memories are summoned and enjoyed once more. Even our summer quarrels and tears are recalled with sympathy and even nostalgia—proof that the glue holds. We

can all recall when the youngest cousin, in his innocent and trusting way, announced that the lightning one starry night was Pa-pa, just letting us know he was there. And we all felt it to be true in some magical, mystical, Percy Quin kind of way. Where else would Pa-pa be but with us?

These are life lessons, indispensable to the next generation: family is messy; love endures hurt; it is only with people you trust that you can dare to risk showing your vulnerabilities and shortcomings, knowing you will be forgiven and loved even more because of it. I sometimes wonder if Malcolm didn't trust us enough to know we would love him no matter what. Or maybe he prized the glue so much he refused to test its strength for fear of hurting us and breaking us apart.

Malcolm, your death has hurt us beyond words, but the glue is stronger, if anything. We need each other more and value each other more. But we would gladly have taken on your hurt if it could have kept you with us. I hug you to me in my heart.

Love always, Mum.

Journal entry—June 14, 2009

I have a song on my MP3 player, *Fix You*, by Coldplay, and I can't stop listening to it. Some songs just touch your heart. "When you love someone but it goes to waste . . ." I don't think it is ever a waste to love someone. For however long and with whatever response, I don't think love is ever a mistake.

"Lights will guide you home . . . And I will try to fix you." It is natural to want to fix someone you love when they are in pain. You would rather be the one hurting than the one watching them suffer. But we can't fix anyone. All we can do is love them and then love them some more, and hope that one day the lights will guide them home.

The Absolute Silence of God
Journal entry—May 26, 2009

I don't remember a time when God was not part of my life. As a child when I got angry that my guardian angel didn't protect me from harm, I didn't reject God. I blamed myself.

I have spent my life in dialogue with God, asking questions, giving thanks, seeking support. I have never heard a response—no visions or voices—but I have often felt God's presence. I have imagined myself being held in God's hands, wrapped in God's arms. I have felt this often enough that the times when I felt the absence of God weren't enough to overwhelm my faith. I wasn't prepared for the absolute silence, absolute absence, absolute aloneness, that followed Malcolm's death.

If there was ever a time when I needed to feel God's presence it was the day after Malcolm's funeral. It was worse than the day we were told he had killed himself. After the funeral there was nothing left to do for him. He was gone completely; I could never see his face again, never ruffle his hair. I desperately needed to sense God's presence, to sense Malcolm's continuing life with God, to feel some confirmation that Malcolm lived on and would be with me in spirit until we could be reunited. It was more than a desperate need; it was a complete and overwhelming need. Beyond words. But a silence descended, a profound heaviness settled on my heart, I was alone. The universe was empty; Malcolm was simply gone.

I wasn't aware of being angry at God at this point, because I didn't sense God's presence at all. This was the time in my life when I most needed God but I felt completely and utterly alone. I know there were people who cared, but I needed the security of my faith. I needed to believe in the possibility of an afterlife. I needed to believe that Malcolm continued somehow, some-where. But his death was like the snuffing out of a candle. After his body was taken away from me and buried in the ground, there was nothing left of him. He was gone; his life was over. Forever.

That was two years ago, and I have struggled with the decision to write about this. I was waiting for a shift in my faith, a rebirth perhaps. But it has been something much more subtle: the acceptance of possibility. Just that. And that will have to be enough for now.

When Children Leave

Journal entry—June 23, 2009

Son number two leaves for the start of his career today. Another loss of a different kind. When I stole a sniff of his abandoned shirt this morning, I didn't have to worry that I would be left with only a lingering musk on his clothes to remind me of him. He is alive and well and will be coming home for the holidays, at least sometimes. And other times we can go to him. As I cried my way to work, it didn't feel much different, less intense but it still hurt. But then every beginning with my sons felt like a loss: their first day with a sitter; their first day at preschool; their first day at high school. And going away to college? I was a weepy mess.

There is no avoiding the pain of loss when you have children. They are always making to leave you: whether it is for their first day in day care or their first day as a professional. But that is as it should be. And if I have done a good job, he will want to come home and visit and not feel the burden of having to.

I love you, my No.1 No2! Be happy, be healthy, be safe . . . and call your mother occasionally.

Anniversaries and Celebrations

Journal entry—March 17, 2009

Two years, Malc. Two years. I wish I could have that last day back so I could tell you I love you one more time and not just, "Bye, have a good day." I wish I could have that last day back so you could skip class and I'd skip work and we'd go fishing and you could tell me how much you hurt.

I wish I could have that last day back so we could go forward together and create a different future, one where you choose to stay and let your dad and me help you. I just wish I could have you back. My sweet son, my first born.

Journal entry—September 21, 2009

Anniversaries don't happen just once a year. They happen every day at 3:30 pm. Every Monday at 3:30 pm. Every 19th of the month. Every March 19th.

For a while every day at 3:30 pm I would pause and have to remind myself to breathe. For at least a year I marked every Monday at 3:30 pm. Now I have moved to every month on the 19th. And this month it was two and a half years. We toasted our son at 3:30 pm on Saturday. That was the time of day when he put a gun to his chest and shot himself through the heart. It still feels strange to be toasting him at that moment, how can one toast a tragedy? But I remind myself of the Irish tradition of raising a glass in memory of a loved one who has passed, and then it makes sense. We live in a permanent state of "waking" our son, in the Irish sense of the word: gathering together to console each other, to share stories about the one who has passed, to celebrate his life and wish him well on his journey. I know Malcolm would approve of the "raising a glass" part.

Journal entry—January 2, 2010

New Year has never been a favorite celebration for Mal and me, and since we have lost Malcolm even less so. This year we stayed home and lit a fire in our outdoor fireplace and drank a glass of wine. I lit some of the candles we had hung outside for Christmas day.

In a way it is sad that I didn't feel sadder. The loss has become the norm, the emotional baseline, and it is more and more possible to have the loss and also be happy. There is less guilt now about the happy moments.

Today we worked on cleaning up the attic. Still some work to do, but we made a good start and took some stuff to Goodwill. Mostly house wares and some clothes. Once the attic has been cleaned, we will be faced with the last remaining major task on our house projects list . . . Malcolm's room. Maybe this year we will start on it. Maybe.

Journal entry—March 7, 2010

We're coming up to three years, and I'm facing the anniversary with trepidation again, but less so than before. I remember how in those first horrific days I wanted only to be with Malcolm; I agonized over the thought that he was

alone and afraid. As weeks and months passed, I felt guilty for abandoning him, for not dying too. As months passed into a year, I fantasized about creating a near death experience so I could see him and hug him once more and make sure he was alright; but I didn't want to die. In my fantasy I would make sure to be resuscitated so that I wouldn't cause my family any more pain. At three years, even that fantasy seems empty, ridiculous even.

Now I wear his jacket to Mardi Gras parades. I read his Facebook page where friends and family still post messages, I look at photos, and sometimes, like today, I help his dad tend to his grave. A parent's nightmare—having to tend their child's grave. But that is the last thing we can do for him now, one last act of love.

Journal entry—May 13, 2010

Tomorrow you would have been 28. So much has changed since you left us. Tomorrow we are gathering with a few of your cousins and maybe a couple of friends. I have baked cupcakes in your honor. You should be there, damn it! We all miss you so much.

Journal entry—June 19, 2010

Mother's Day, Father's Day, the celebration of parenting. For Mother's day the grammar school usually had the kids make special presents. Father's Day was always in the summer, so it got short shrift. I feel bad about that, but the boys and I usually did a pretty decent job ourselves. We did have a good tradition of having special breakfasts together on the special days . . . birthdays and such. And now that the boys aren't home with us, it is a bit of an effort to keep that tradition going. But we each deserve our special days, so Mal and I try to make an effort with birthdays, but Mother's Day and Father's Day just don't work anymore. Yet we do, it nonetheless, each one trying to get the other through their day. Spending time with Mal's mother helps because it gets us out of our own heads, at least it helps me. I hope it helps Mal.

Malc, you need to help your dad through tomorrow. Help him remember the many, many times he was a good dad. Help him be kind to himself. He misses you so much, and he's so hard on himself.

Tracing His Steps
Journal entry—April 19, 2010

This year on Good Friday my husband and I made our own way of the cross: we walked to the site where Malcolm shot himself three years ago. We walked to the corner where he parked his car. We walked across the open lot that he crossed to get to the lakefront. But up on the levee there has been construction, so we can no longer place our hands on the soil that absorbed his blood and add our tears to the ground that held him as he died. Perhaps that's a good thing.

I am not prone to quoting scripture, but I am reminded of the Book of Revelation,

> *"And God shall wipe away all tears from their eyes; and there shall be no more death, neither sorrow, nor crying, neither shall there be any more pain: for the former things are passed away. And he that sat upon the throne said, Behold, I make all things new."*
>
> Revelation 21:4-5a

It gives me comfort to think that God has taken my son and made all things new for him. It's a good thought today, and I am in need of a good thought. A new levee represents strength and safety and protection. Malcolm would approve.

Was the Universe/God Sending Me Help?
Journal entry—June 6, 2010

Even as I begin to write, I am filled with trepidation, because I adamantly don't believe that everything happens for a reason or everything works out for

the best. I don't believe that God has a Plan and that we are just acting out a pre-written script. There is no sense to these notions in the face of the abuse of children, natural disasters, plagues, evil, and injustice.

But as I prepare to say goodbye to a colleague, I must admit to having had a revelation of sorts. Then as I re-read a posting from May, 2008 I realized I had felt this way for a while.

God's Grace

I held a baby at work today. A co-worker had his infant son with him. The baby began crying and I held him and stroked his face and hummed, and he took his pacifier and was content. He relaxed and then he slept in my arms. It was such a joy to hold that child; I wasn't helping a co-worker I was helping me. I felt my heart heal, if only a little, and I felt a joy that I haven't been able to feel all year.

New life is such a grace, such a sign of hope. It was OK that I had to hand him back because in laying my hand on his face somehow God had laid her hand on my heart.

Billy was hired within a few months of Malcolm's death. He was right out of college, and I got to watch him grow into his first professional position. The next year he became a dad, and I got to babysit a little. I am not saying that God sent Billy into my life, but I'm saying that looking back I see how Billy helped me to heal. I have been able to mother him a little and that felt good. And then I was able to mother his baby a little, too.

Now he is leaving, and it hurts. But I am aware of the gift that he has been in my life, and I wanted to acknowledge that. Is it God closing a door and opening a window? No! God wasn't responsible for Malcolm's death; God didn't close that door. But maybe God has been trying to help me let go.

I have cried a lot in the last couple of weeks as I worked on a photo collage and memory book for Billy. I have been angry . . . having to lose a "son" all over again. But I'll be okay. I am more ready now than I was three years ago to let go. And Porp has a new baby, and James is coming to Flint Creek. There is a lot to be thankful for. And maybe, just maybe, God has been with me all along.

The Journey of Grieving

Journal entry—April 27, 2008

Grief affects us all in different ways; my husband sighs constantly. I wanted to point it out to him and tell him how annoying it was, because it always makes me feel like I have done something wrong. How self-absorbed to assume it was about me. He's just trying to breathe; sometimes that's about all one can do. And sometimes even that takes an effort.

The evenings and weekends are tough. I lie on the sofa, and it feels as though something heavy is on my chest, and if I don't consciously choose to breathe it feels as if my body will quit breathing altogether. I felt crazy until someone in my support group said they have the very same sensations. Anxiety can do that, apparently.

Journal entry—October 10, 2009

Grief often feels like an emotional rollercoaster. There aren't real "highs" so much as incredibly intense moments of joy when one recalls and shares a memory, a story, an event. But such joys are a double-edged sword. As intense as that moment of bliss is—that crest of the roller coaster—the intensity of the following fall is magnified exponentially, as the realization of the loss hits one's psyche like a punch in the gut. And like a rollercoaster ride that goes through a pool of water, you are left feeling breathless, submerged in sadness, wondering if you will have enough energy to complete the ride, enough air to take you through to the next stretch of track.

Journal entry—June 12, 2010

As I sat through the Cantor's last synagogue service last night (when I wasn't running to the bathroom to blot my face and rehydrate) I realized that this

was more than about a friend leaving, I realized that grieving a loss is something that you revisit when another loss occurs. Billy isn't my son, but my grief over his leaving has become exacerbated by my ongoing grief about losing Malcolm. So this is about Billy, but it is also about my other loss. Truth is, when my pet bunny rabbit "Pretty Girl" dies (she's already 11 years old) I will probably grieve excessively then, too.

Maybe it is the heart's way of surviving a profound loss. It isn't possible to feel all the grief associated with the loss of a child at one time, or in one season of grief, and so, when your life moves into a new season of grief because of a new loss of some kind, your heart gets in touch with some of your original pain and helps you release and process a little bit more.

Once I understood this I was less judgmental about my tears and more compassionate towards myself. I actually let myself cry, and it was ok. I didn't die, and no one laughed at me, or got angry, or over-reacted as if I needed emotional triage: they just let me be and later just checked in with me and asked if I was ok. And . . . I was. Sad, damp, but basically okay.

Journal entry—May 18, 2013

Each time we face a trauma, the same responses to grief have to be navigated. Whether it is the loss of a house in a storm or the loss of faith. Whether we suffer the death of a loved one or the death of a relationship. We can't just learn these lessons once and for all and refer back to them, like reviewing for an exam. We have to live through them all over again—every awful emotion, because each loss, while creating similar emotional havoc, is intrinsically different.

Does knowing what to expect about the nature of grief help as you navigate through the emotional mine fields of loss? Well, not really, at least not at the time. But looking back after a period of time has passed, you can gain some perspective, and it becomes possible to discern the journey you have already taken. You discover that you have travelled some distance in your grieving. You realize you are not in the same place you were, even if you thought nothing had changed. Becoming aware of this progress can feel good. But it can also feel like betrayal, because you are letting go. When you realize that life is becoming more bearable, you feel simultaneously that you are moving further and further from the one you have lost.

After his death I felt so far from Malcolm, so separated, and so angry about it. I couldn't accept that I would never touch him again, smell his clothes, muss his hair, or hear him laugh. There had to be something, something I could do. It couldn't just be over . . . his life. How could that be possible? There is no way to put into words the complete frustration and rage when you realize absolutely nothing can be done. You are helpless. Events move forward and you want to scream, Stop! Stop! And then slowly, imperceptibly, you begin to accept your loss.

Now, after six years, I somehow feel closer to him than I did that first year. Once I moved towards acceptance of the loss, I was able to stop fighting it. I was able to let go of some of the anger and then, it seems, I was able to make room for Malcolm again in my heart. Now I don't feel the same separation I felt that first year. It's not that I sense him with me in a supernatural way so much as I am able to recall how much he was a part of my life—and still is. It has been a long journey to reach this place of partial peace and there have been cycles of deep and dark grief and depression along the way. But each time I have worked through the darkness I have become stronger and the loss has become easier to bear.

Letting Go

Journal entry—June 8, 2010

Last night I threw out a jar of olives from the fridge. They were out of date by three years and looked a bit like a science experiment. Olives were never meant to be fuzzy. But it was still hard to throw them out because they were Malcolm's. Silly, I suppose, but there you are. Mal paused too.

You know we can't keep everything as a souvenir.
I know, I know.

I am pretty sure he was thinking about the one inch of rum left in a bottle that was Malcolm's, and how he is not ready to drink it or throw it away. But we take baby steps. Yesterday it was olives.

Journal entry—March 20, 2011

Grief, like spring cleaning, is all about baby steps. Last week I decided to sort through a drawer in Malcolm's desk and made piles, what was important enough to keep and what I was willing to part with. And then my husband sorted through the discards and pulled out a map of Austria—Malcolm spent his last summer there, and a pair of nail clippers—Malcolm cut his nails with those. I know that might seem silly—nail clippers. But after those first horrific hours passed and it began to sink in that we would never see him again, I collected his hair from the drain in his shower; if I had found nail clippings I would have kept those too. You can't understand unless you have been there— and may you never be there.

It has been four years, as of yesterday. Four springs when we have asked ourselves, are we ready yet? Is it time to finish cleaning out his room? Timing is very delicate here. When my husband washed my son's sheets a few weeks after he died, it nearly put me back in the hospital. How could he decide to get rid of any of Malcolm's smell? How could he? I was hysterical, hardly able to breathe through my sobs. Now only traces of his musky odor linger . . . a camping jacket, a knitted cap. And our younger son's friends have slept in Malcolm's bed during Mardi Gras visits, and I have replaced the sheets.

Going forward there will be hundreds of decisions to make. Every article of clothing, every note, every memento. His desk contains fragments of the life of the boy and of the man, from grammar school to graduate school. Every one of them precious, every one of them a tenuous connection, every one of them holding out the elusive hope of an answer. What if there's a letter hidden between pages of a book, a note in a pocket? Some revelation of a broken heart or a paralyzing fear. But did he really know why, on that day in March 2007 just three hours after handing in a paper to his professor, he took a gun and shot himself through the heart? I'm not sure any more.

I think this spring what we need to let go of is our need for an answer. Maybe then we will be able, finally, to let go of Malcolm's things. But not this year. Not yet.

Making Peace with Life
Journal entry—July 10, 2010

O Life,
How oft we throw it off and think,—'Enough,
Enough of life in so much!—here's a cause
For rupture; herein we must break with Life,
Or be ourselves unworthy; here we are wronged,
Maimed, spoiled for aspiration; farewell Life!'
—And so, as froward babes, we hide our eyes
And think all ended.—Then, Life calls to us . . .
Still, Life's voice!—still, we make our peace with Life.
         —Elizabeth Barrett Browning, "Aurora Leigh"

I read this today in a used book in a second-hand bookstore, so I came home and looked it up. It is strange how we can come across answers we aren't looking for in places we weren't planning to be.

Life can call to us when we are at our lowest point, ready to give up, but maybe the call doesn't come in time. Or maybe some are just not able to respond to life with hope. There were some days in the past three years when I felt, "enough, enough of life," but I somehow managed to keep moving, keep breathing. Now I feel my response to life is, yes. It doesn't feel like I am being disloyal to Malcolm any more to choose to stay here. I suppose I am making my peace with life.

The Storm of Stress

Journal entry—August 29, 2010

I recently came across a very useful metaphor about Post-Traumatic Stress, comparing it to the level of water in a river. Dr. Scott Coffey, a University of Mississippi Medical Center Researcher, studied Katrina-related PTSD in lower Mississippi where flooding is a very real threat. He concluded that in the same way a single afternoon rainstorm can cause flooding in an already swollen river, so too even a relatively minor stress can trigger a crisis if you already suffer from PTSD; your river (of stress) is always running high.[1]

Surely the same can be said for those who suffer from other mood disorders. People who struggled with depression before Katrina were less able to weather the psychological effects of the storm. Suicide rates tripled in areas along the coast, and that is only an estimate. Many suicides go unreported as such.

Was Malcolm a victim of Katrina? Not in a direct sense, maybe, but I am sure Katrina was one of the currents in his river of stress and anxiety. After the storm he worked for contractors gutting houses; he walked in the debris of people's lives every day. In January, 2006, when the University of New Orleans opened up again, he drove to his on-campus job, and to class, through the devastation of Lakeview. Day after day he saw evidence of the precariousness of life and the elusiveness of safety in a community at the mercy of the weather.

As he came to the end of his course-work for his M.A. he had to face the fact that he was moving into adulthood and independence. However much we tried to assure him of our constant support, however much we slowly walked him through the minutiae of adult financial responsibilities, however often we tried to convince him he was already a really good tutor and youth mentor and would make a great teacher, I now think that perhaps he was slowly drowning in his fears and insecurities. As if he saw his future like Lakeview—a place of hopelessness.

---

[1] "Gulf grapples with mental health issues after Katrina." By Pam Firmin—McClatchy Newspapers. Printed in the *Columbus Ledger Enquirer*, Thursday, August 26, 2010.

So, perhaps Malcolm was a storm victim, and Katrina was a part of that storm.

His last moments alive were at the lakefront, a place where, before Katrina, he had always found comfort and calm, and that is where he chose to end his life. I only hope that in his last breaths he found that elusive calm he had so desperately sought for so long.

Today the Younger Brother Became the Older
Journal entry—September 10, 2010
One of the joys of having a child who loves math and problem solving is that he can work out complex computations. Some things, though, maybe shouldn't be discovered, like the very day on which you have officially outlived your older brother—counting leap years and everything. Today, James tells us, is that day. As of 3.30 pm he became the older brother. I don't know how to get inside that experience with him. But then again I don't think I should. Some griefs are personal.

So, on this day of passage, I want to write a letter to my second child.

You were a great younger brother. Malcolm knew how much you wanted to be with him and be like him and be included by him. Although he got aggravated by your following him physically and socially, somewhere inside he was kind of flattered to have a fan. He loved you even while he ganged up against you with TJ; he knew he would always have you. When he grew up, he became so proud of you.

As you get your head and heart around the significance of today, remember that the life you live does not have to somehow be valuable enough to compensate for Malcolm's death. The only life you have to live is your own; the only expectations you have to live up to are your own. You have nothing to prove to us. We are already proud of who you are and what you have accomplished.

I am sorry Malcolm isn't here for you, leading the way into adulthood and parenthood. But you are not alone. You have us, and you have a big extended family. Stay ever closer to your cousins no matter how far you go geographically. Remember, family is the glue (!) and you can still be "Uncle" James to Beth's twins.

We love you.

No Longer Afraid of the Dark

Journal entry—April 3, 2011

Recently, I had an epiphany. After a lifetime of being afraid of the dark, and of being alone in my own home, I am no longer afraid. And it is because of Malcolm. No, I don't believe in ghosts, but I have always been nervous about an empty house and easily spooked by noises. Too many bad experiences at night as a child, probably. But recently, when I heard the shower door close by itself with a bang as it does when the metal rim cools down, I guess, I smiled to myself and thought, maybe that's Malcolm just letting me know he's here. And I suddenly felt safe. Silly, I know, but nonetheless I have felt less nervous in the house ever since that moment.

It has been four years since Malcolm's death, and if he had wanted to haunt us, surely he would have done so sooner. So I am sure this is more about me coming to terms with his death than about him actually deciding to make himself present to me. After four years that would seem a little tardy on his part.

It's hard to get my head around the fact that it's been four years. Some days it seems as if it was just last year, as if we were going through the first calendar year without him. But no. It has been four years. I couldn't have started my book without the passage of those years. It was necessary for the immediacy of the pain to lessen. It was impossible to put anything into words those first few months. Even in my journaling and in sessions with my therapist, I couldn't bring myself to use the word "dead" except to express my guilt about not being so myself. But now I find myself speaking of Malcolm in the past tense more easily. I have even said, when meeting a stranger, that I have one son. I still think that is tantamount to a lie, but sometimes it is just not necessary to go through the whole story if you know you will likely never see that person again. Sometimes it's okay to give yourself an emotional break. I know Malcolm would understand and smile, *It's okay, mum, I know you haven't forgotten me.* As if I ever could!

Seasons of Loss

Seasons of loss
each year another
but each year is different
scars have become body art
the pain is part of who we are
integrated
assimilated
yet it aches in a deeper way as the season approaches
like arthritic joints at the approach of rain
and somehow the ache is welcome
we know they will not be forgotten

Surviving the Suicide of a Child

Journal entry—May 21, 2011

Psychologists suggest that the loss of a child is the greatest loss an adult can experience, greater than the loss of one's parents or even one's spouse. Little comfort. But I suppose it means that if I can survive this, I can survive. Period. And there is some comfort in that. Four years ago I didn't believe my survival was possible. After a year I created a blog and wrote about surviving the loss of my son. On that blog I posted Malcolm's eulogy, which I have included in this book, with my husband's and son's permission. Eventually I was able to write about the day Malcolm died. I couldn't do that until I began to forgive myself for not following him into his darkness and making sure he would never be alone. I still struggle with that, especially around the anniversary of his death, but I am stronger now and more committed to my life.

Committing to life was no easy thing for me. Reading accounts of other parent's acceptance of their child's death and their immediate renewal of faith would make me angry. I found no easy grace in his death. But to be fair to these other parents, Malcolm's death was a suicide, so the reaction is much more complex than just the loss of a child. The use of the word "just"

here seems callous and dismissive of the excruciating pain that accompanies the death of a child, and I don't mean to be dismissive. But when there is a loss due to a disease or an accident, or even a murder, it is possible to point to the immediate cause and to identify, if not completely understand, the causal chain of events that led up to it. It doesn't make it easier to answer why these events were "allowed" to happen in our God-created universe, but it is something.

When there is a suicide there is a large gaping chasm in the causal chain that there may be no way of bridging. Even if there is a note, the contents of that note may make no sense or may offer no explanation, just a profession of tender love. Malcolm told us he loved us. He told us he knew that we loved him, that it wasn't about us. It was about him, that it had always been about him, and we could have done nothing to prevent his death. But how could he say that when he hadn't given us a chance to try?

One of the most difficult things for suicide survivors is trying to figure out why. For the first few months Mal and I thought about it and talked about it obsessively. Trying out new theories with each other. What did we miss? Debating endlessly in our heads if not out loud what we could have done differently, what part we played in his pain. Wanting to ask his friends and his cousins if they knew anything that would shed a light on Malcolm's decision, but not wanting to cause them more pain by asking.

This past year Mal and I have spoken less and less about it. The fourth anniversary was a beautiful day, so we drove across the lake and had lunch and more than a few beers. We toasted Malcolm at 3:30 pm and shared our story with a couple of strangers in a neighborhood bar in Mandeville, one Malcolm would definitely have approved of. We all cried into our drinks and bonded in the way one can with complete strangers you will never see again. They gave us hugs when we left the bar. Then we walked and sat by the lake and watched a boating regatta. Eventually we had coffee and began to catch each other up on our thinking about Malcolm's death. Our theories were different, but there was less intensity in our differences. It has become clear to each of us that we

will never know, and we are beginning to rest with that reality a little. Just a little. But that's something.

PTSD and the Experience of Loss

When I lost my oldest son to suicide, my therapist had to put on a new hat: grief counselor. And I am so grateful that she was willing to do so. When you suffer from Post-Traumatic Stress Disorder, the experience of another trauma exacerbates all your symptoms. Recurrent nightmares have been one of my symptoms since early childhood, and any stress event tends to give rise to them. Malcolm's death resulted in nightmares about children dying. Night after night in my dreams I would meet infants and toddlers who were sick or hurt, and I would try to get them help. But they always died. I think the issue I was dealing with was powerlessness: I couldn't save my son's life. And that powerlessness played out in the nightmares. I still have these nightmares on occasion.

Another symptom of PTSD that became intensified in the grieving process was having panic attacks. Prior to losing Malcolm it was not uncommon for me to have a panic attack during Sunday Mass in a Catholic Church. I would be overcome with fear and feel as if I was in imminent danger. Then would come the shaking and crying, and we would have to get up and leave. After Malcolm's death the panic attacks happened in a grocery store we shopped at regularly. As I reached for his favorite pop-tarts I would remember he was gone, and I would be unable to breathe. In a clothing store he liked, I would look at T-shirts he might have worn and find my legs going weak, and my stomach lurching. There are still restaurants we have been unable to return to. During the panic attacks I would often have an intense feeling that there was something I still needed to do to save Malcolm. Something I had forgotten that would fix everything. As if I could, by an act of will, turn back time and resolve history in a different way. What was it, what was it? Breathless, weak and clammy I would have to sit down on the floor and put my head between my knees. Episodes of panic become more intense as the anniversary of his death rolls around. Even now after seven years, I am aware of increased nightmares leading up to March 19th.

Something closely associated with PTSD is dissociation. Most simply put dissociation is "spacing out." We all do it. When we drive on automatic pilot, for instance, and suddenly find ourselves halfway to work without clearly remembering taking the right turns. Dissociation[2] as a disorder is just a more exaggerated version of that kind of experience. For me, dissociation has meant experiencing emotions and reality from the perspective of the scared child I once was. Sometimes I will look at my hands or look in the mirror and not recognize myself. On more than one occasion Malcolm helped me through bad days of dissociation. He would be patient and sit with me and watch movies, or drive me to the store.

This inner-child me looked at Malcolm as her hero. And when he died I discovered a level of grief coming from this child-self inside. My internal Little Mona was angry that Malcolm had abandoned her and sad that he would not be there to rescue her any more. An aspect of grieving for me now had to involve tending to the emotions coming up from this place inside. I needed to do some serious self-parenting, which I worked on in therapy and in my hospital stays.

Allowing myself to express the anger was a big part of the self-parenting process. This felt strange because in my adult mind I was not angry at Malcolm, although being angry would have been normal. No, my anger came from Little Mona. My expression of the anger was therefore very child-like: I drew pictures, wrote letters, imagined myself with Malcolm in my safe place enjoying his company. I was a child with her big brother. But there turned out to be a dark side to this. During one major bout of depression in 2013, it was

---

[2]Dissociation is a common defense/reaction to stressful or traumatic situations. Severe isolated traumas or repeated traumas may result in a person developing a dissociative disorder. A dissociative disorder impairs the normal state of awareness and limits or alters one's sense of identity, memory or consciousness.

—Marlene Steinberg, M.D. "In Depth: Understanding Dissociative Disorders"
http://psychcentral.com/lib/in-depth-understanding-dissociative-disorders/0001377

the inner child me who became insistent on being with Malcolm and seeing him again. This intense desire expressed itself in the form of suicidal thinking.

Dissociation and loss can be very complicated and, for me certainly, could not be safely navigated without therapeutic help. But with the care and support of an excellent therapist, and the loving and constant presence of my husband, I continue to work through it safely.

FAITH, HOPE, AND MAYBE GOD

In the hope of hope.

No Easy Grace

Journal—November 21, 2011

Looking back on some of my more recent reflections I see a tentative hope that the idea of God may still have some meaning. Perhaps it's simply that I am slowly healing from the loss of my son, and I am experiencing a space opening up in my heart for the possibility of God.

During the Katrina months I felt God's presence; as I struggled for years with the burden of sexual abuse, I felt God's presence. But then there was the absolute silence of God that followed Malcolm's death. What was different about that experience of loss? What changed—me or God? And is there something new happening now?

I find myself wondering, was it God's hand that had held me all along, supporting me through my losses? I know that I am grateful that I found the right therapists at the right time, making sure I received enough therapy to survive the next major loss in my life. And I am grateful that I left teaching when I did, and my students weren't exposed directly to the effects of my son's suicide. I am also grateful for the Jewish community where I was given the space to mourn, while people held me close with their compassion and affection. Were these gifts the presence of grace in my life? If my whole journey has been an experience of grace, then there is indeed no easy grace.

I'm not sure I expect any answers any more, but I believe that the questions of God and faith and meaning and grace are the most important questions anyone can ask, and that the pursuit of these questions and their potential answers continues to be the most important journey of my life.

It's Only Human to be a Mess

A definition of the whole human person includes body, mind, and heart, experience and expectations, goals and dreams, and also all the messy stuff: anger, remorse, despair, doubt, fear, and lots of uncertainty. But the definition of the human person has not always been this inclusive. In the conclusion of *Irrational Man*, philosopher William Barrett credits existential philosophy with bringing the whole human person, the total mystery, into the context of philosophy. This approach to philosophy is in contrast to other modern philosophies that tend to define the human person primarily in intellectual terms.

Barrett writes that is it vital to acknowledge our darker side. We may not want to admit to the darker aspects of our Self—the anger, the uncertainty—but Barrett cautions against denying the existence of this darker side, what he calls "the furies." According to Barrett modern society is intent on doing just that: encouraging us all to flee from the shadow side of the Self and thereby deny our full nature. And he suggests that we do so at our peril, because like it or not the furies are real, and happy and healthy adults must find a way to integrate them into their lives.

Barrett's insight about the messiness of the human person is somehow comforting. It's not news to me—I am completely aware of my darker side. But he officially lets me off the hook regarding being perfect; he says that to be human is to be imperfect, to be unsure. I don't have to pretend to be certain; I don't have to worry about why I worry so much. I don't have to experience an epiphany, or discover the 7 Secrets Of . . . success, or weight loss, or a fulfilling postmenopausal sex life. I can accept that I'm just a mess and keep on working at being a little less so. Thank you Mr. Barrett!

But Why Doesn't God Fix the Mess?

Theists claim we are created in God's image, the high point of God's creative enterprise. Does the fact that the human self can be such a mess belie that belief? Or perhaps God isn't the perfect, omnipotent, all-knowing, unchanging Being of Christian theology. If we stick with the classical view of God, we have to find a way of reconciling the problem of suffering—especially innocent suffering—with a God who has the power and foreknowledge but not the desire, apparently, to stop it. But what if God is not the All Powerful Being with a Plan?

In his book *Original Blessing*, Matthew Fox suggests that part of our spirituality should involve going deeper, not just reaching higher. He equates the journey into the depths as an embracing of the dark side of reality, of ourselves, and even of God. Pema Chödrön, a Buddhist nun, writes that befriending the darkness, the anger and the pain in our lives, is the way to peace. She also writes about the need for compassion towards those who hurt us as well as towards ourselves.[1] For Chödrön, and many other contemporary religious writers, compassion should be embraced as a way of life.

I wish Barrett, Fox, and Chödrön were all wrong, but I am wondering more and more if they are right. Religion and faith aren't just about peace and salvation and comfort and "Joy to the World." Of course not, I know that. Every sane adult knows that life is more complicated than the scenes depicted on Christmas cards. And yet we resent suffering and pain and assume that these are aberrant, not part of the Divine Plan, if there is indeed a Plan. But what if it is part of the Plan, at least in the sense that it is simply part of the way life is, and God is the source of life, so it is part of the way God made life to be. Can we live with that? With the fact that life hurts, and God knows it hurts and seems to be okay with that? With the fact that life is unfair and good people do suffer sometimes more than evil people, as Harold Kushner and the biblical Job uncomfortably remind us? Do we have a choice? Not if we want to keep religion and faith in our lives, it seems. If that is indeed what we want.

Harold Kushner in *When Bad Things Happen to Good People* suggests that when God chose to create, it was necessary for God to be self-limiting. For creation in general and humanity in particular to be separate realities from God, it

---

[1] *When Things Fall Apart: Heartfelt Advice for Hard Times*, Pema Chödrön.

was necessary for God to pull back and relinquish control. So, in terms of the Problem of Evil we discussed earlier, God is indeed not all-powerful in relation to human behavior or the workings of the natural world. But even if God is not all-powerful it doesn't mean that God doesn't have a Plan, it just means that as people make decisions and natural events happen, the Plan has to be adjusted to the next best possible scenario—the next best of all possible worlds.

My son took his life. I cannot believe that was part of a Divine Plan, how could it be, if we define God as Goodness. What Malcolm did was exercise his (God-given) freedom. So now, what is God's Plan, what does God hope for? God surely hopes that everybody who is touched by Malcolm's death manages to survive and make nurturing, compassionate decisions about their own lives and relationships. More than this, God must hope that we learn to appreciate all our blessings and gifts even more. The blessings and gifts we experience every day; the miracle of life on this planet of ours.

Intelligent Design and the God Particle

The issue of God's Plan has become part of the dialogue between science and religion. Scientists point to the evidence of the profound waste and destruction of life involved in human evolution, and in human conception. The death of so many species; the loss of so many lives—if indeed every fertilized human egg is a life. If this is the Plan of a so-called Intelligent Designer, they muse, God doesn't seem either very intelligent or particularly compassionate. But does science have a better answer than the God answer?

Science can provide answers that religion cannot: the How rather than the Why of life in the universe. But, if you look into science more closely, you discover that there are some very basic questions that science is still grappling with. How is the universe shaped, for example, or what is the nature of time, and are there multiple universes? And who or what lit the fuse for the Big Bang, metaphorically speaking? Then there is the issue of the "One Theory." Scientists have been trying to reconcile the theory of general relativity—the theory we have used with great success to explain how things work on the large scale—with the theory of Quantum Mechanics, which explains how things work on a submolecular level. So far they have been unable to, and that is no small matter (pardon the pun).

Religion and science; religion versus science. Is there one universe or many? If there is a God, is God the God of all universes? If God is as theism traditionally describes God, then, yes, there can only be one Supreme Being. If so, are there other universes with other beings made in God's image? You know, like how all the aliens in the Star Trek series look human with a few extra nose ridges or forehead bumps. In fact, I think there was a Star Trek story-line to the effect that the same "Being" had seeded various locations in the universe. But Star Trek aside, does it really matter if there are multiple universes? All we have for sure is the universe we know. Can't we leave the rest to speculative cosmologists and theoretical physicists?

That might work if some physicists kept to their own corner (and their own language and paradigms) and didn't keep claiming to have explained the origins of the universe without recourse to a God. In the opening episode of the show "Curiosity" on the Discovery Channel Stephen Hawking claims to have done exactly that, explain the origins of the universe scientifically without needing to posit the existence of a divine creator. Apparently subatomic particles can just appear, seemingly out of nothing and from nowhere. Our universe began as a tiny particle according to astrophysicists, so perhaps it too just appeared and was not, after all, created.

I'm not sure how convincing this argument is. Perhaps the issue is not the appearance of particles "ex nihilo" (from nothing) but the inability of humans to see where these particles were before we were able to detect them. After all, when I was in grammar school no one knew about quarks. Evidence of their physical existence was first noted in 1968, and they've been around, apparently, since the Big Bang. Just recently scientists claimed to have detected the Higgs Boson particle for the first time. This particle is nicknamed the "God Particle" because it apparently holds the answer to many fundamental questions about matter. But until recently its existence was just a theory.

I'm not against science; science is incredible. As much as I understand it, science seems to be doing a good job explaining the micro- and macro-cosmic realities. Nonetheless, scientists don't get to tell me about God. Even scientists as credentialed as Hawking. If I decide I don't believe in God, I want to arrive at that conclusion myself, not be forced to find my answer looking through the lens of particle physics.

A Holy, Different God?

Working in a synagogue provided me with access to a wholly different (I would also suggest "holy/different") view of God. I borrowed books from its library and picked the brains of two different rabbis in the congregation; and along the way I discovered a way of relating to God that was a refreshing change from the Parent/Child relationship of traditional theism, with its anthropomorphic images of God. Instead of describing God using the titles that fill the Hebrew Scriptures—Father, King, Judge (even Mother in a few instances)—Reform Judaism is more likely to use descriptions that express God's unique and very nonhuman role as Creator and Sustainer of the universe.

In general, Reform Judaism is characterized less by the rituals of Judaism and more by an emphasis on the improvement of society and the eradication of injustice and social evils, *Tikkun Olam*, "healing the world." In fact, in my experience, involvement in social action is more common in the Reform community than participation in Shabbat (Sabbath) services. Service not services!

One of the most influential Jewish voices in the first half of the twentieth century, Mordecai Kaplan, moves even further away from traditional biblical descriptions of God. In *The Meaning of God in Modern Jewish Religion*, Kaplan suggests that God is not a "Being," but neither is God simply a philosophical abstraction. God is *"the sum of the animating, organizing forces and relationships which are forever making a cosmos out of chaos."* Kaplan describes God as the creative life of the universe and suggests that we become holy when we express that creative urge. Instead of talking about Mercy and Justice as qualities of God, Kaplan describes Mercy and Justice as divine in themselves. To believe in God, he suggests, is to believe that "human life is supremely worthwhile." For Kaplan, God is the worthwhileness that underlies life; and when we are helping to make life more worthwhile for others, we are doing something innately holy and God-like.

Kaplan is describing God in a radically new way, refusing to create God in our image, the way traditional theism has always done. Instead of using metaphors such as Father (and Mother), King, Judge, Warrior and the like, Kaplan pushes our God-language beyond metaphor and analogy, and away from its tether to the human experience. Does this make the concept of God more or less accessible, though? As a parent myself, I have found the parent image of God very insightful. But there was always the problem of suffering and punishment. Why would a loving, all-powerful God allow His or Her children to suffer? Was it enough to say that God didn't send the suffering but entered into it with us? Perhaps. But Kaplan presents an alternative, and one that doesn't end up in the conundrum presented by the Problem of Evil.

Kaplan's approach offers me a sense of relief: God isn't my Father, (or my Mother); I don't have to place myself in the psychological role of a child in order to relate to the Divine. But this new way of thinking about God is also daunting: sometimes (often) it is comforting to think of the Big Daddy in the sky. I totally sympathize with Ricky Gervais' character in the movie, *The Invention of Lying*. He made up the concepts of the "Big Man in the Sky" and a beautiful "Heaven" because his mother was dying in profound fear of the nothingness that awaited her. And when people heard this "lie," they immediately accepted it as true and overwhelmed him with questions about how to get to heaven. They wanted simplistic answers and foolproof rules. I cringe at the element of truth contained in this satirical portrayal of religious faith.

People hope for, even long for, something other than the life they have, and if their life is full of pain and sorrow that is understandable. However, the life we have is the only reality we can be sure of, and projecting our hopes and expectations of happiness into a future life after death distracts us from

appreciating the life we have, and the need to work at making our lives worthwhile, and the lives of others more bearable.

Can we maintain a hopeful outlook in a universe that doesn't offer the security of a Divine Designer, Author of the Great Plan, Architect of History? Is this concept of The Holy enough for us to anchor ourselves to, to have faith in? And what about the millions who still cling to the Cosmic Santa Claus? Is it the duty of the "enlightened" to break the rose-colored faith spectacles of the religiously naïve? Some college philosophy professors seem to think it is, but are they right?

I don't believe that anyone should attack another person's faith and religious naïveté. If someone's faith provides a structure of meaning that makes life doable, then she has a gift that cynics might secretly long for. No one has the right to debase another's view of God or to impose her own—whether atheist or Pentecostal fundamentalist. Those who try to do so are being spiritually violent; we all have our own spiritual path to walk and deserve to do so in our own time. And the cynics can no more prove the nonexistence of God and ultimate futility of life than religious believers can prove the existence of God and the ultimate purposefulness of life.

In the Christian tradition we are used to thinking about God as a Being, as a relational Someone. We use metaphors such as King, Shepherd, and Father. But perhaps, as Kaplan suggests, God is not a Being; perhaps God is the "Ground of our Being," as Lutheran theologian Paul Tillich suggests. Or maybe just "Being."

In Hebrew the name for God YHWH (Yahweh) is associated with the verb "to be." In the Book of Exodus when Moses asked God, "Who is it that I shall say is sending me?" God answered: "Ehyeh asher ehyeh,"[2] which, because biblical Hebrew verbs have no tense, could be translated in many ways: *I will be what I will be. I am that I am. I am all that is.* One inference is that the author of Exodus believed God to be the Source of all, indeed the very "Ground of our Being" as Tillich names God.

---

[2]Exodus 3:13-14.

Jesus and the Ground of Our Being

The author of John's Gospel uses the phrase "I am"—the basis of the word Yahweh, the Hebrew name for God—to frame seven sayings of Jesus. They are referred to as the "I am" sayings. One example is "I am the Way the Truth and the Life." The use of the phrase "I am" in these sayings serves to remind the reader of the name of Yahweh and hence infer the divinity of Jesus.

It seems clear that John's community had come to believe in Jesus as the incarnation—"*enfleshment*"—of God. John also describes Jesus as the Word (Logos) of God, a popular concept among first century Jewish writers. But it took the Church five hundred years to figure out a way of defining the relationship of the Father and the Son: One Godhead, Three Persons. The trouble with Jesus was that he was just too real, too substantial; how could he be the Transcendent Creator and also the Ground of our Being and still be this guy from Nazareth?

Who did Jesus believe he was? The only title that scholars agree Jesus used for himself was Son of Man. A title that could simply mean human or could refer to a Jewish figure that prophets said would come directly from God at the end of time. But if Jesus was cautious or coy about his identity (or perhaps just unsure), he was very clear about what he wanted his followers to do. Jesus asks Peter three times, "Do you love me?" and each time when Peter responds in the affirmative, Jesus instructs him to "tend my sheep." Jesus was a teacher, but what he taught was a way of life, and he didn't just talk it, he lived it. The triple repetition to Peter is a universal oral storytelling technique. I am sure you can call to mind stories and jokes with triple repetitions. Repetition is a way of helping people remember something important. Have you noticed all those annoying commercials on the radio that repeat 1-800 numbers three times? There's a reason for paying for those extra seconds of air time: repetition works. A friend shared a story about an old southern preacher who when asked why he was such a good preacher replied, "First I tell them what I'm going to tell them, then I tell them, they I tell them what I just told them."

The point is Jesus was making a point (or the author of John's Gospel was making a point about Jesus): if you love me/Jesus, do something to express that love in action on behalf of others. If Jesus is to be understood as God's Word, then the message is clear. God wants acts of justice, just like Amos preached hundreds of years before Jesus. Nowhere in the Gospels does Jesus say, "If you love me, worship me." Christianity seems so often to miss the point on this. By focusing on God as *a* Being and on Jesus as *a* Being, we lose sight of what Jesus was about: Doing.

Jesus was the Doing of God

Forget the debates over the language of Trinity and Incarnation (Substance and Person) in the early centuries of the Church. The Jews and the Taoists have it right: God is the unnameable, and it's pointless to try to name the unnameable. If we name God, God becomes a thing, and therefore less than God.

Forget creating God in our own image through anthropomorphisms like Father, Mother, or King. Forget arguments over who is saved or whether there is a heaven, or if vampires are evil spirits (does holy water work better than garlic, I can never remember). Instead, how about focusing on Doing God or maybe Doing Goodness.

And for Christians, we shouldn't worry about who Jesus was. We know that he was—Jesus bar Joseph, (bar means "son of" in Aramaic), or Jesus of Nazareth. What is more important is who he became: he became the presence of God. The next question is what is his significance for us? Paul has the right idea when he tells his converts: "Now you are the body of The Christ."[3] He is telling Jesus' followers, *you are his hands and his feet. So go be Jesus to others.* Maybe this is the best understanding of the resurrection, or maybe just the easiest to make sense of: The Christ (Messiah) is here with us only in so far as we, his followers, incarnate him (make him flesh) through living the way he

---

[3] I Cor. 12:27.

would have lived—in the way we treat others and engage in the world professionally and personally—challenging unjust systems and laws, advocating for the oppressed, feeding the hungry, attending to the sick, forgiving sinners, forgiving ourselves!

Resurrection or Hallucination?

The resurrection of Jesus is such a central piece in the faith of Christians, is it enough to speak of it metaphorically, to say that Christians are the continued presence of Jesus in the world? And if Jesus' resurrection was more about an experience of the resurrection of hope and courage among the Apostles than about a bodily resurrection what does that say about belief in life after death?

Below is an inner dialogue with "Jesus." Not the real Jesus but rather my inner attempt to know Jesus. Like my conversations with Oprah, they are totally imaginary, but sometimes I gain important insights in these dialogues.

Saturday, March 5, 2011

(Me) Resurrection or Hallucination? This is the crux of the issue isn't it? The whole conquered death thing.

(Jesus) I suppose you could say that.

Well, wouldn't you say that?

I have always thought, hoped, that my life would be more important than my death. That what I said and did, or tried to do, would have more of a lasting impact on the world than what was done to me.

And what was done to you? Was it really a sacrifice to appease God?

There was an ancient practice of blood sacrifice among many peoples. The destruction of the Temple put an end to it for the Jews.

155

So the end of animal sacrifice was a good thing?

It was time for that to end; the Pharisees were right on that point. All you have to do is look at the beginning of the Jewish Scriptures. They got it right in those stories. The Word of God has the power to create life itself from nothing, why would God need animal bloodletting in order to be "satisfied?" It's a very barbaric, primitive concept, don't you think?

I do. I totally do. But in the minds of the ancients there was the assumption that what humans did could manipulate the gods and hence reality. Through dance, song, reenactment of hunts or battles, and through sacrifices, they thought they could change outcomes, control the future. They thought they could bring rain, guarantee fertility of wives or crops, determine victory in battle. And then when people started to believe in one, supreme God, they assumed the same held true.

You are right. But there is more to it than that. As the belief in a stern but compassionate Father/God became the norm for the Jewish faith, Jews tended to attribute to God the same characteristics of their own tribal leaders and fathers. Sons want to prove themselves to their fathers in deeds of glory and courage, and so they assumed God the Father would want the same homage. Jacob chose well when he chose the thoughtful leader, not the bloodthirsty hunter to lead his tribe. But the Hebrew people still wanted kings and heroes like their neighbors. So God became imaged as a king too.

So there is a lot going on here: ancient cultural norms, family dynamics, traditional pagan religious beliefs, and not a little social and religious patriarchy.

Indeed. So it is easily understood that people who believed in me wanted to believe my death was part of the whole plan. They wanted to understand it as the moment in human history when animal sacrifice became obsolete once and for all, the ultimate and final blood sacrifice had now been made, God's

Son had "satisfied" God's need for justice, atonement, vengeance. Don't you see the context? How this message was vital if the Jews were to believe in me?

You've lost me.

The Jews lost the Temple in 60 CE. No more sacrifice was possible therefore no more ritual atonement. But if you looked back thirty years to my death and interpreted it as the final sacrifice, then it would seem that this was God's plan all along, that we don't need the Temple any more. What did Paul write—the body is the temple of the Holy Spirit, and I was the final High Priest.

Theologically then, to see your death as a blood sacrifice, as THE blood sacrifice, it was important to connect your death to the destruction of the priesthood and the Temple. And all of this would be seen as part of God's plan. It makes logical sense. But of course most Jews didn't accept this interpretation and didn't become followers of Christ. And the Greeks who came to dominate the church just accepted the sacrificial interpretation of Jesus' death.

The ancient Greeks had their own traditions of sacrifice to their gods in their mythology, so the idea of my death putting an end to the need for pagan sacrifice also worked.

We've been carrying this blood satisfaction theology for 2,000 years. Don't you think it is time to take you down from the cross?

Ah, which brings us to the resurrection. Which I think was your initial question. Power over death; eternal life. These are so often the core issues of religions. Who or what has the power to conquer the natural cycle of life and death and offer people an everlasting life. Where is the fountain of youth? Is there another level of existence where humanity lives on? I wonder, is it fear that motivates this preoccupation humans have with conquering death?

Perhaps, but as a mother who has lost a child I want to add that it is love, too. Anyone who has lost someone dear to them would naturally be excited at the possibility of seeing him again, and would want to believe, would hope, that the dead loved one is experiencing some form of happiness that perhaps eluded him in this life because of illness or circumstance. So, maybe it is fear, yes, but also love and hope.

In fact, I have been reading about grief and about how people who are grieving commonly have hallucinations of the one who has died. And I was wondering if maybe the resurrection appearances were hallucinations of that kind?

So you don't believe in the resurrection?

I'm not saying that, exactly. I'm saying that the stories in the scriptures may be about grief. Mary Magdalene, the key witness, loved Jesus—loved you—profoundly, and in her grief she sought out the tomb to anoint you. I can't imagine how it would have felt to her to be about to touch the dead body of her beloved, her leader, her savior. I couldn't have anointed my son without it breaking my heart all over again. I would have wanted to stay in the grave with him. Mary Magdalene would desperately have wanted to see you alive, to reverse the events of your death. For me, as for Mary it seems, it was the morning after my son's burial that the reality of the loss really hit for the first time. I know that desperation.

So you think there was no empty tomb?

I don't know about the tomb, I just know about grief.

Is it possible that the grief was real and the empty tomb was real? Or do you fight that possibility because you never "saw" your son after he died? Are you still angry that he never appeared to you and said, *Everything is ok, mum. I'm alright?*

That's a low blow.

> I truly am sorry for your loss and your pain. But might it be possible that there
> was a resurrection, that there is life after death, and it might be possible that
> your son is, indeed, okay, even if he has not told you so himself.

> I had a dream of Malcolm once where he told me he was okay, and I
> thought there would be many like it. But, looking back, there was just that
> one. Which makes it more significant, now, I suppose.

> And what did he say in that dream?

> He was smiling his big, joyous smile. He told us he was hanging out with
> friends and we shouldn't be worried about him. It was a great place, and he
> was fishing. I woke up smiling.

> And now?

> Now, looking back, maybe it was more than just an ordinary dream. Or
> maybe I just want it to be.

> But it turns out it was special, unique even.

Yes, it was.

> So?

So maybe I keep hoping—for life beyond life, love beyond death.

The Nature of Faith

"*I think therefore I am*," Descartes famously wrote. Because I am aware of myself thinking about myself, I must exist. Thanks Descartes, that's a start. I don't

have to have faith in my existence, I have proof. People often place proof and faith in opposition. If there was proof that God existed, we wouldn't need to have faith; if there was proof that God existed, rejecting the concept of God would be irrational. But there isn't proof, so does faith require that we suspend all intellectual enquiry and accept everything without question? The act of questioning the existence of God or the validity of religious doctrine is equivalent to heresy for many religious people. Yet theologians John Westerhoff and James Fowler present theories in which doubt and questioning are part of the process of faith development. It certainly seems to be a common trait of adolescents and college students.

What is faith, exactly? Is faith a relationship with God, or is it a set of intellectual beliefs? The Bible contains a variety of views on faith. Among both ancient Jews and early Christians there were those who reduced faith to religious rituals and others who reduced faith to verbal expressions of belief. Prophets and Apostles spoke out against this reductionism, preaching that neither empty ritual nor vacuous blessings constitute real faith. What was more important, they said, was justice.

"I hate, I despise your religious feasts; I cannot stand your assemblies . . . Away with the noise of your songs! I will not listen to the music of your harps. But let justice roll on like a river, righteousness like a never-failing stream!"

Amos 5: 21-24

"Anyone who listens to the Word [of God] but does not do what it says is like a man who looks at his face in a mirror and, after looking at himself, goes away and immediately forgets what he looks like."

James 1:23-24

"My brothers, what good is it to profess faith, without practicing it . . ."

James 2:14

"Woe to you, teachers of the law and Pharisees, you hypocrites! . . . you have neglected the more important matters of the law—justice, mercy and faithfulness."

Matthew 23:23

The Catholic Church has been criticized for its overemphasis on the rubrics of correct ritual, and for its zealous commitment to ancient laws—regarding the role of women, for example. A resurgence in practices such as benediction and Eucharistic adoration is seen by many as a move back to a more magical or superstitious attitude to religion.

Pentecostal or so called "born-again" Christian denominations have been criticized for their overemphasis on "professing" Jesus as one's personal savior as the basis for salvation and then ignoring or underplaying the necessity of a committed moral life, even going so far as blaming moral lapses on the devil and not the individual.

Is faith a matter or beliefs, a trusting relationship, or moral action? Head, heart, or hands? In the preceding quotes James was concerned with faith as belief in action: walking the walk not just talking the talk. Amos and Matthew, on the other hand, were concerned with the quality of the action: acts of justice and mercy, not pious, empty ritual.

The nature of Christian faith has been debated since the New Testament times. Faith was the theological crux of the Luther versus Rome debacle in the 16th century which resulted in the Reformation. Although usually explained as the result of Luther's (very understandable) disillusionment with a corrupt papacy, the theological agenda of the Reformation was faith alone versus faith and good works as the road to salvation. Was faith in Jesus enough, or could one earn salvation through good works—in particular the good work of buying indulgences and thus releasing sinners from punishment after death in the form of Purgatory.

Sensible Protestants and Catholics, including Luther (himself originally a Catholic priest), believed that living a moral life was a necessary response

to the gift of God's saving grace. Moral license was not what Luther had in mind. His issue was the type of good works—not empty, superstitious, financial transactions, but acts of justice and mercy: we need to be Christ not buy off Christ! Sadly, the Vatican didn't give Luther a hearing, and hence the Reformation resulted. One of the greatest tragedies in Christian history.

What do I conclude from this historical survey, if anything? For one thing, some Catholic bishops aren't doing a lot better than Church leaders in the sixteenth century in terms of living lives of moral integrity consistent with their stated faith. But the lack of congruity between the words and deeds of Church leaders shouldn't be an excuse for abandoning my faith in God. Unless I believe that the hierarchy really does represent God, and I don't. Because if they do represent God, then God is a God of materialism, hypocrisy, child abuse and endangerment, moral depravity and deceit. And if there is indeed a God, God is certainly not any of that.

Faith in God has to involve more than spoken words, more than external rituals. Faith in God cannot be dependent on religious leadership; it has to involve one's whole life, one's ongoing struggle to have a relationship with whatever kind of God one believes in. Otherwise faith is just a role we act out on Sundays.

Faith and Religion—What's Age Got to do With it?

According to a 2008 survey by the Pew Forum on Religion and Public Life, 88% of American adults are absolutely certain or fairly certain about the existence of God. On the other hand only 39% attend weekly services, and another 33% monthly or yearly services. Of those who attend services, I would suspect that some adults may be attending out of a duty to raise their children in the faith they were raised in, even though they have no personal confidence in their religion. Others may be fulfilling their duty to drive their housebound elderly parents to services.

I sometimes wonder if my issues with the Catholic Church are a factor of my age and not a reflection of the state of the Church. Catholic liturgies seem to be attended by young marrieds with small children in preschool through 8th grade, and senior citizens. Where are the middle-somethings—those of us with teenagers or college age kids, those of us with working kids and recently emptied nests? Is it our age or our stage in life that keeps us too busy or makes us too ready to criticize the institutional Church? Perhaps I am too easily disillusioned now, having been around long enough to personally know members of the clergy and witness their inadequacies. Or do I have a hard time hearing "wisdom" preached to me by someone the age of my own children? In the movie *Gran Torino* I found the relationship between Clint Eastwood's character, Walt Kowalski, and his pastor, Father Janovich, a very realistic portrayal of this latter dilemma.

Father Janovich, eulogizing Walt,

Walt Kowalski once said to me that I knew nothing about life or death because I was an overeducated, 27-year-old virgin who held the hand of superstitious old women and promised them eternity.

I remember my father and his Irish Catholic buddies. They would drive their families to mass on Sunday, sit in the back pews while their families went further up the aisle, wait until people sat for the homily and then leave out the back door and head for the pub across the street, returning only to drive the family home. My dad's expressed view of the priest's (any priest's) homily was, *"Who the hell does he think he is telling me what to do. He's no better than me!"* I think dad and Walt would have gotten on famously! Yet my dad ended up singing in a church choir with my mum, when they were both in their 80's. Maybe he had become more tolerant of imperfection, both in himself and in his clergy.

Religious faith and religious practice aren't synonymous. Perhaps our attitude to religious practice is affected by our age, or at least by our stage in life. At certain points in our life we may practice a religion out of duty, but eventually, if we are to be genuine about our religion, it has to become a

personal commitment. At that point what we believe and what we practice need to achieve some congruity. And the "practice" piece needs to integrate our ethics as well as our religious behavior: the whole person not just the Sunday observer.

A Faith Development Theory

There is a theory of faith development that human development theorists usually reference. The author of the theory is James Fowler and his faith development theory suggests growth in steps and stages. According to this theory moving up to a higher stage of faith involves leaving behind different beliefs and behaviors. But the faith development theory I found more applicable to the lives of my students and to my own experience was that of John Westerhoff, as presented in, *Will our Children Have Faith?* (1976). Westerhoff compares faith development to the way in which a tree grows, each ring building on and adding to that which has grown before. Faith development is seen as "adding to" something we already have, rather than as moving on or letting go of "childish ways" from earlier stages of development.

According to Westerhoff doubt, trust, childlike joy, and mature intellectual assent can all exist within an adult person's faith life. To doubt is not to lose one's faith, far from it. Having doubts is natural, just one flavor in the gumbo that is our faith life. Westerhoff makes no judgment about the type of beliefs we have—liberal or fundamentalist—and if we are fundamentalist our faith is not judged as immature, as it would be according to James Fowler's better known theory.

At the core of Westerhoff's faith "tree" is our earliest exposure to religion, the *Experienced* style of faith. As a child or as a convert in a new faith tradition, we receive the faith from those who nurture and mentor us. Then as we grow, we learn the prayers and traditions and go through initiations—what Westerhoff identifies as the *Affiliative* style of faith. If we are born into a religion, we may not have much choice in our affiliation. My students often complained that Confirmation into the Catholic Church had been their parents' choice.

Or that their Catholic grammar school didn't allow for anyone to "opt out" of Confirmation class. Interestingly, I witnessed the same disaffection among adolescent Jews preparing for their Bar or Bat Mitzvah in the Reform tradition. Rituals of passage do not necessarily involve a personal choice, it seems, more often participating in such a ritual is the result of family pressure. Yet at some point faith has to become a choice, or it really never becomes our faith.

In Westerhoff's understanding of faith, questioning, experimentation, and doubt have their place in faith development in the *Searching* style of faith. For James Fowler doubt and questioning signify a shift from one stage to another. In other words doubt is part of the faith journey and not a sign of losing one's faith. This view of doubt makes sense to me and corresponds to what I have witnessed in the lives of my students. If we don't question, how can we choose to believe or trust? If we just imitate and follow, then we are simply "drinking the Kool-Aid," acting like faith lemmings walking off the cliff of credulity. Taking on religious faith without questioning anything is not a sign of maturity. In my view a healthy Catholic is someone who has examined the historical flaws of their church and their popes, and the changing nature of their doctrines, and has made a reasoned commitment to the religion not because of religious authority but, perhaps, in spite of it. The same view of healthy religious commitment applies to all Christian churches and non-Christian traditions.

The culmination of faith development is a personal, *Owned* faith integrated into one's life not compartmentalized into an hour's duty on the weekend. Adult converts to a religious faith often have more interest in and commitment to the rituals and doctrines of a tradition than those born into it, because as converts they have searched for and now take ownership of their faith. For people born into a religious tradition, it may not be until marriage and parenthood that the issue of choosing one's faith becomes a pressing issue, and even then adults may be choosing an educational system not a religious faith *per se*. Many adults never achieve this style or stage of faith development, attending church out of a sense of duty to one's family, or a concern with public opinion, or maybe a need to garner votes if they are running for political office.

But even achieving an owned faith doesn't mean we have absolute certainty about God. Westerhoff suggests we will more likely continuously move between the rings on our faith tree, processing, questioning, enjoying, rejecting . . . but all from the perspective of adult "ownership" of and commitment to our faith journey. So perhaps where I am with God and faith is just "on my journey." Maybe I am where I should be.

In God's Image?

William Barrett and John Westerhoff have provided me with lots of good news: not only can I affirm that it is natural to be a mess, I can also affirm that having doubts and despair is not equivalent to losing my faith in God and is certainly not proof of God's nonexistence. I'm normal it turns out, and that's quite a relief. But it's also kind of a disappointment. I was hoping for a little bit more of something "spectacular, extraordinary, unique" in my personal *Self*. But perhaps I am extraordinary, too. What do I mean by my Self? There is generic human nature which we all share, and then there are the specific selves we each develop, and that is where we are unique.

Let's examine this issue of human nature for a moment. Assuming that there is a Divinity/God, let's put aside the notion of God "creating" humanity in a *fully developed, this is exactly how we were intended to be*, kind of way. After all, the scientific evidence for the development of species and for the genetic connectedness between species is hard to deny. If we have evolved then, like all of creation including the planet Earth and in fact the whole universe, we are still evolving—or at least changing (I'm not sure we are improving). And if we are still changing, how can we say that Human Nature as it is NOW is what God created or intended. Or NOW, or wait . . . NOW! You get the point.

Then the question arises: if we are made in God's image and we are still changing, does that mean God is still changing? Is changing human nature reflecting changes in God, or is our changing understanding of God the result of changes in us?

Human Development and Hope

Another lens through which to view and understand my faith journey is that of psychology. Psychologist Erik Erikson identified eight ages of psychosocial development, each with its own particular challenge expressed in the form of opposites. From the ages of about 40–65, which is my current stage, the challenge is *Generativity versus Stagnation*. Facing the major changes of the empty nest or the lack of children (and for women the end of one's ability to ever have children) and heading towards the middle of one's life expectancy, we are apt to ask ourselves: *Have I created something that will outlast me?* As a mother, the loss of a child is especially traumatic at this age because you are no longer capable of bearing other children. So, while some of the issue of my despair and lack of hope may be due to my stage in life, a lot of the cause is specifically the loss of my child.

Yet my despair didn't begin with the loss of my son. Erikson suggests that the very first psychological challenge in human development, from birth to eighteen months, is to overcome the conflict between trust and mistrust. If one manages to grow in a healthful way and overcome the conflict basic to the *Trust versus Mistrust* stage then one gains the virtue of hope—each of Erikson's eight ages is associated with a virtue. So, building trust and learning hope are foundational to the development of a healthy self. Moreover, if this task of developing trust is incomplete then the conflict carries over into the rest of one's life, as do all unresolved issues from each successive age.

As a child I experienced abusive treatment by adults in authority over me, adults I should have been able to trust. And I did not receive the nurturing and affirmation so necessary in childhood. The absence of this nurturing was tragic (though sadly not uncommon) and I grew up with an inability to trust, and with doubt, shame, and a lack of hope. All of these are the effects of an inhibited psychosocial development during the first six years of life, according to Erikson. Children who are abused carry that damage with them in the form of unfinished developmental tasks. Despite love, family, and much personal growth, I have a deep sense of mistrust and despair that lingers inside me

psychologically. This is why a new loss brings up the emotional detritus of past losses and a new trauma initiates a recycling of old trauma.

And now, where am I headed next as I move through the eight ages of human development? The *Integrity versus Despair* stage, according to Erikson, occurs late in adulthood, from age 65 to the end of one's life. So that will be my final stage. At this stage people look back and ask, *What have I done that has any meaning? Have I made a difference? How will I be remembered?* Parenting has given my life meaning, as has teaching, and now writing. Sharing my story will perhaps make a difference for someone in his or her journey through grief and loss. And that gives me hope.

What About Bob?

Journal entry—December 3, 2011

For at least two years after Malcolm's death my flower beds languished in varying degrees of weeditude. Sometimes I would make an effort to tidy them up, but as to actually taking care of any of the plants, not so much. My gardens had to make do with whatever nourishment the skies provided, and in New Orleans, especially in the summer months, that can be a feast or famine experience. I lost quite a few lovely friends: Rosemary, Rose, Petunia.

Occasionally, I would take pity on a malnourished specimen and, instead of digging it up and throwing it away, replant it in the back yard, where it could die without disturbing the neighbors or causing me public humiliation. Sometimes these replants would do better in the shaded back garden under our "family tree" or along the fence. In time a sort of triage flower bed developed. I even rescued a neighbor's discarded rubber plant from their trash. I figured it deserved another chance; my triage bed was a better proposition than the local dump. But once the rescued plants were in my back yard, they were pretty much on their own.

The rubber plant froze at least three times and came back strong and insistent. I think it was just plain stubborn. I also had a houseplant that didn't like my house. It too had frozen and been re-born more than once. But this past winter was too much for both of them. My husband and I dug them both up, feeling like neglectful parents. We didn't immediately put them out for the trash, it not being pickup day, and a couple of days later, when I went to retrieve them, I noticed a tiny green growth on the root of my houseplant. It's alive, it's alive!! So I carefully trimmed the giant bulbous root and placed it back in its hole trying to make it comfortable. I had nearly trashed a living thing. Oh, the guilt! Later that day my husband was cutting the grass and had a déjà vu experience looking at the root that was once a plant. Forgetting that we had already dug it up he went ahead and dug it up. Again!

When I saw Bob . . . he now had a name . . . in the trash bin once again, I got a little hysterical. What was Mal doing? Didn't he see Bob was alive? How could he abandon Bob like that? Mal was just a little perturbed by my (over) reaction. But came to understand what I was saying (hollering), and Bob was gently re-replanted. I put bricks around him so that Mal wouldn't forget and mow him over the next week. Bob was at a very sensitive stage, only just beginning to grow shoots—there were now two visible—and they were very delicate.

Needless to say, I became a more attentive gardener after that episode, and Bob is now sprouting every which way and has grown to be about two feet. He is still far from his previous healthy height, but he is coming along nicely. I find that plants actually do respond to daily watering in the summer months (who knew?) although some are more forgiving than others.

So, why call him Bob? Well, Bob taught me a lesson: even when things appear to be hopeless, there is always the possibility of new beginnings—of Hope. Thanks, Bob (Hope).

Feeling Spiritually Bereft

Journal entry—December 30, 2011

I have been searching for different ways to name and understand God. For Jewish rabbi and educator Mordecai Kaplan, God is the *Worth-while-ness that underlies life*, and when we are helping to make life more worthwhile for others we are doing something innately holy. For Lutheran theologian Paul Tillich,

God is likewise the *Something beneath and throughout reality . . . the Ground of our Being.* While this very immanent view of God may suit a postmodern, existentialist approach to life and reality, it leaves me feeling bereft. I want the something above and beyond, not just underneath it all. I want the Great Wholly Other, the Big Something Else. Am I in search of a Cosmic Bigfoot? Is this search based on my psychological inadequacy, or am I expressing an innate yearning of the soul that is restless until it rests in God, as Augustine once wrote?

I think God is more than an underlying source of meaning; I think there is more to God. In fact, I wonder if we don't risk trivializing the discussion of God and Meaning, of God-Talk, if we don't look beyond our immediacy to . . . if not another reality such as Heaven, or Oneness with the Divine . . . at least to a higher Ultimate Value, Ultimate *Something Else.* I'm not just looking for a greater depth to reality but something more than reality as we experience it. I don't want to believe that there is no Reality beyond my perception of reality. I don't want to settle for life as we know it, or even a bit better than we know it; I don't want the superficial to be all there is. I don't have to believe in life after death to satisfy this need, but I do have to have a Meaning beyond meaning, a Love beyond love, a Value beyond value.

Come on . . . all you're doing is capitalizing words. What does that mean? It doesn't make things more significant or more real.

Maybe not. But it signifies that I'm not done yet, that I am still searching, still looking beyond. And maybe that's all I have right now.

If You Don't Care About God Can You Still Find Meaning?
Journal entry—February 12, 2012

Maybe you don't care about Jesus. Maybe you are not sure about God, and discussions of God's nature seem pointless. Perhaps the notion of faith has no meaning for you, and you're not sure if there is any ultimate "Meaning" to life or the universe. So why bother "being good" or "working to make the world a better place?" A reasonable question.

I could say that doing good is a good thing to do. Period! But again, why? If you don't buy into altruism, then how about selfism? Doing good can make you feel better, or at the very least distract you from focusing all your emotional energy on the detritus that is your life. Bit harsh? Sorry! But it does work: if you want to feel better, stop focusing on how much life sucks. In fact medical science is providing more and more evidence that practicing positive thinking and resolving our anger with forgiveness reduces anxiety and stress and in turn reduces instances of heart attacks.

In the pursuit of a meaningful life, having a meaningful job helps, I have found. Working in a job or industry that does not at least claim to be about improving the human condition, in a local or global context, would be difficult for me. Education was a meaningful job, and so is working in a synagogue. In the synagogue I work with a team of professionals dedicated to nurturing people on their faith journey—from birth to death. I know, I've said I'm not sure about God, and I'm not. But I am sure that bringing people together to give thanks for life's gifts, to acknowledge and respond to people's needs, to celebrate life's passages, to mourn life's losses is in itself both important and meaningful. Working in a synagogue and assisting with the religious education program helps to give my life meaning. It's not my faith of origin, but it is faith.

In *Man's Search for Meaning,* Viktor Frankl wrote that helping people find meaning gave his life meaning. That sentiment helped me remain committed to religious education even after the Boston abuse revelations in 2002. It has also motivated me to write, and in the last few years it has given significance to my work in the synagogue.

How to Respond to Change: Who Moved My Cheese and Replaced it with Manure?

Spencer Johnson, the author of *Who Moved my Cheese?* makes some excellent points about how people react to change. In his story, miniature people called Hem and Haw, and two mice called Sniff and Scurry, live in a maze and hunt for cheese. When the supply of cheese runs out, Hem denies this new reality

and stubbornly refuses to adapt, preferring to believe that his cheese supply would one day be replenished and life would be as it always had been. So he sits in an empty Cheese Collection Station waiting passively for cheese to magically reappear, refusing to face the fact that his life has irrevocably changed— that the cheese will never come back; life will never by the same again. Hem has suffered major losses: safety, predictability, comfort, sustenance. And each time he has responded with denial. Then he loses his best friend Haw, who strikes out on his own in search of new cheese.

Hem is like any one of us on whom a whole pile of existential manure has been dumped. We are so angry, so indignant: How could it have been dumped on us? How could the universe or God or Karma mistakenly think we deserved it? There has to have been a cosmic mistake, we tell ourselves, and we fully expect the mistake to be rectified and everything to return to normal. Even though logic and science and countless friends and self-help books tell us that such a reversal of fate is unlikely, we sit and wait. Eventually the smell of our manure becomes our new normal. Then our friends stop coming by, tired of their advice falling on deaf ears, and really tired of the smell! Our denial turns into depression, and self-pity becomes self-destructive.

When it gets to this point, we really need to consider burying the manure in a garden and doing some relandscaping. Then we can have our friends over for a barbeque. My mother was right: don't focus on the stink of the horse manure (she gathered it from the horses that passed our house) that life deposits outside your door, go shovel it up and put it on your roses. My mother had the best looking roses on our lane.

Here's my favorite manure joke:

Twin boys wake up on the morning of their eleventh birthday to see a huge mountain of horse manure in their back yard. One twin looks out the bedroom window with disgust and says, Typical! Nothing good ever happens on my birthday. The other brother leaps to his feet and rushes outside, grabs a shovel and starts digging.

The first twin shouts down through the open window, *Jeez! What the heck are you doing? Are you nuts?*

And his brother answers, *No . . . with all this shit there has to be a horse in there somewhere.*

Okay, so maybe there is no pony inside your particular pile of manure, but maybe you can take the manure and grow beautiful roses like my mother did, or start a vegetable garden and sell your produce in a local market, then save the money and buy your own pony. There are options. That's all I'm saying.

Here are some suggestions:

- Don't worry about the *Why* of tragedies such as natural disasters, evil, innocent suffering, or loss. Whether there is or isn't a God, suffering still happens.
- You can waste your whole life trying to find a satisfying answer or "satisfaction" in the form of retaliation or redress, but forgiveness is healthier—forgiveness in the form of letting go. It is possible for abusers to die and never admit their guilt—as they did in my case, making it even more important for me to let it go.
- Focus on the healing—your own inner healing from anger, grief, and sadness, and the healing of others in the community in which you can make a difference.
- There is great wisdom out there. Make a point of bringing some of this wisdom into your daily living.
- Every day is both a gift and a challenge.

Faith in a Silent God

Our God so frequently does not respond to our call. Our God does not appear on demand. We are struck by God's absence in times of acute trauma . . . [In such times] *What does matter is where we choose to cast our lot.*

Traces of God, Neil Gillman

Traces of God is an anthology of reflections organized around four theological themes, one of which is the experience of the presence of God. Gillman, a rabbi and professor of Jewish Philosophy at the Jewish Theological Seminary in New York, relates the story of Elijah's contest with the prophets of Baal. In this story Elijah calls on Yahweh to show the powerlessness of the god Baal. In response to Elijah's prayer, Yahweh sends down fire to light a sacrifice, something that the prophets of Baal had proved unable to do. An impressive experience of God indeed. But was the miraculous intervention of Yahweh the basis of Elijah's faith? Gilman suggests not, speculating that, even if God had not responded, Elijah would have remained faithful: his faith was an act of trust.

For most of us there are no burning bushes or shooting flames. Our experience is probably more comparable to a later story about Elijah when he is in a cave hiding from those seeking to kill him. Elijah prays for God's help, but God is not to be seen or heard from in any loud and powerful force of nature. Instead Elijah strains to hear God's whisper in a gentle breeze and has to convince himself he is not alone. It is here that Elijah's faith is truly tested—alone in the cave, feeling as if he has been abandoned by his God. It is then, in his time of greatest need facing the apparent absence of God, that his faith really becomes a choice.

I have felt that absence of God's love, that heavy, airless silence that accompanies despair. Angry and alone I have damned the God I no longer believed in, daring a reaction from a nonexistent deity. But even God's anger was silent. Now that my anger has dissipated, I wonder if I really wanted a divine sign. I'm not sure I would have known how to deal with hearing God, or seeing God in a sudden conflagration.

In the end, finding traces of God may be more about a choice to see something divine in the ordinary rather than an experience of an extraordinary event. And if we choose not to believe in God, then what? Gillman asks, if not God, then who or what else are we going to choose to believe in that will lend coherence to our lives? Who or what indeed!

Still Searching

Since "blessing" is the theological word for "goodness," original blessing is about original goodness. The forces of fear and pessimism so prevalent in society and religion need to be countered by an increased awareness of awe and goodness. The goodness is inherent in the beauty, wisdom, and wonder of creation. Goodness and creation go together as do goodness and God. As Meister Eckhart put it, "Goodness is the proper name of God the Creator." When creation becomes the starting point of spirituality once again, then hope will return also. We will see everything differently, including Divinity itself. This blessing awareness will motivate us to hopeful—and generous—actions.

—Matthew Fox, *Original Blessing*

Originally published in 1983, *Original Blessing* was reissued in 2000, garnering renewed support from those who read it over twenty years ago and capturing the imagination of a whole new generation of spiritual travelers. In a wonderful moment or circularity for me, the new preface makes reference to the writings of Pema Chödrön, a Buddhist nun whose work I recently discovered.

I keep coming back to the theme of Creation-Spirituality—the view represented in the quote above—perhaps as an antidote to the traditional Christian focus on sin, suffering, and the cross. But can Creation-Spirituality survive the theories of multiple universes and the Big Bang? Can we sustain the belief that the original nature of the world and of humanity is good and a reflection of The Good/The Creator God, in the light of science's insistence that there is no rhyme, no reason, no Intelligent Design?

I think we have to focus each on our own "universe," the orbit of our own lives. Then we can ask, what signs of wisdom and beauty, wonder and order do we find there? And is it enough evidence for us to choose to trust in God and Goodness?

A Different View of Spirituality and Evolution

I believe Matthew Fox was right when he denied the "Fall of Man" theology in favor of something more positive: Original Blessing instead of Original Sin. And what if the evolutionary theory of Pierre Teilhard de Chardin was right: we are (the universe is) evolving towards an ever greater perfection, god-like-ness, oneness with God, an Omega Point.

If we accept an evolutionary view of creation, humanity, and spirituality, it would mean that what we have now, and what we are now, is but a shadow of what we are capable of and what we will one day become. And if we accept this view, our vision should be outward, looking into the universe and reaching out and ever forward. The evolutionary view makes me excited about living and about the future of humanity; it makes me hopeful. I find joy and hope in imagining something greater than, beyond, and in front of me, calling me to be a better human being, calling me to leave a positive footprint in the human community and on the planet.

Do I have to name that Beyond, that Omega Point as God? Do I have to worship on bended knee? I like to garden. I bend my knees when I garden. That, for me is a kind of worship . . . tending the earth, giving thanks to the soil, creating (attempting to create) beauty for others to enjoy. My Druid brother would approve, I think.

What About Finding God Within?

I have talked before about Ultimate Values. There are many that one can name, such as Meaning, Goodness, Beauty, Mercy, Compassion, Justice, and Courage. These Ultimate Values can be seen as something to strive toward, something above and beyond. But they can also be recognized within us, at least in nascent form. In naming ultimate values I am naming something outside of my experience of self, something that I am called to, inspired by, motivated by, but also something that I have experienced within. I have recognized them in the world around me as values worth defending, sharing, and supporting, and I have recognized them in the behavior of others as values worth emulating. But I have also experienced them as a yearning coming from within myself to be something more than I am, to create something of value with my life, to make a positive difference in my community. These values are like seeds sown in the human heart; human imperfection drawn to that which is Perfect. Perhaps God is the source of these values in a theistic sense, or perhaps the values are simply aspects of Divinity, that which is divine.

Does this mean that Plato was right, we are drawn to a higher world of Perfect Ideas or Forms, of Moral Ideals? No, Plato believed this world was the shadow world, the Cave. I don't see it that way, although there are things that keep us in the dark. Ignorance, narrow-mindedness, fundamentalism, hatred, bigotry, I-am-right-and-you-deserve-to-die-for-not-agreeing-with-me-ism, these things are our human cave. But we don't have to live in that cave, we can reject the darkness. We don't have to wait to move beyond this life to experience a more perfect world, we can shine a light on our small-mindedness and see its ugliness for what it is, and then decide to live differently.

When we experience a discomfort, a nagging dissatisfaction with who we are and how we are living—our lack of commitment to ultimate values—we are experiencing an opportunity for growth. We can choose to embrace this dissatisfaction and work at changing ourselves for the better, or we can find comfort by surrounding ourselves with people who are more imperfect than we are. By doing so we ignore the invitation to personal growth and therefore for a more meaningful life.

Wisdom From a Buddhist Nun: Pema Chödrön

Pema Chödrön is a Buddhist nun who runs an abbey and writes about the spiritual life. I don't know about you, but I didn't know there were female religious in Buddhism. It was a happy discovery. I find her ideas both comforting and challenging, and what I love the most is that she is both a voice of religious wisdom and a woman. I know that sounds genderist but it is important to me, right now, to discover wisdom in the voices of women. Her ideas break me open. I find her words full of truth, yet she makes no claims to speak for

The Truth, to be anything other than a spiritual traveler who is willing to share what she has learned from Buddhism. You don't have to accept Buddhism to recognize the truth of her words, and for someone like me, healing from the wounds of the Catholic Church, her words are a balm.

It is Pema's teaching on compassion, a concept that underlies her whole philosophy, that has had the most impact on me. Respond to people with compassion, she writes, including—in fact most especially—those who make us angry and those who hurt us. This teaching is familiar because it is exactly what St. Paul tells his followers about becoming Christ, we should become the hands and the body of Christ; we should be Christ's compassion.

What does it mean to become Christ? I've heard it my whole life but have I practiced it? Turn the other cheek, offer food to the hungry, healing and compassion to the sick and to the sinner. Pema Chödrön, a once Christian now Buddhist nun, has discovered a universal truth and Buddhism has shown her a way to live this truth in a way that Christianity, for whatever reason, did not.

God / Goodness / Godness, whatever we name it, is made immanent by us becoming more than we are, becoming an embodiment of universal values such as Compassion. God is of course more than this. We haven't defined God but we have made a connection with something tangible, something livable, doable.

Discovering a path doesn't mean that I have all the answers. The principle of compassion offers no explanation for evil and suffering and I still struggle with all the old doubts and guilt and anger. Pema Chödrön also readily admits a continued struggle of her own. I find that comforting. Let me allow her to explain:

Let Go of the Idea that You'll Ever Get It All Together

The very first teaching I ever got that I can remember was at a dharma-dhatu, one of the centers Rinpoche established. One of the older students was giving a talk, and he began by saying, "If you are interested in these teachings, then you have to accept the fact that you're never going to get it all together." It was a shocking statement to me. He said with a lot of clarity, "You are never going to get it all together, you're never going to get your act together, fully, completely. You're never going to get all the little loose ends tied up."

Life is so inconvenient. It's so inconvenient running this abbey, I can't tell you. You just get the kitchen together and the bookkeeper leaves. You just get the books together and the housekeeper leaves. . . .

But in wholeheartedly practicing and wholeheartedly following that path, this inconvenience is not an obstacle. It's simply a certain texture of life, a certain energy of life. Not only that, sometimes when you just get flying and it all feels so good and you think, "This is it, this is the path that has heart," you suddenly fall flat on your face. Everybody's looking at you. You say to yourself, "What happened to that path that had heart? This feels like the path full of mud in my face."

—Pema Chödrön, *The Wisdom of No Escape*

Reprinted by arrangement with Shambhala Publications, Inc., Boston. www.shambhala.com.

Recognizing Grace

What is grace? I have used the word before, but I haven't explained what I understand it to mean. The word derives from the Latin *gratia* meaning "gift." Christians traditionally talk about faith and salvation as gifts, as underserved and unearned graces from God. But then the question arises, why is it only some individuals receive these gifts? The issue becomes even more complicated when you factor in the whole non-Christian community. And then what about atheists and agnostics? Isn't God the God of all? And if God is like a parent, how can any of the children of God be rejected for choosing to believe differently. That's not how a loving family behaves. Even crazy Aunt Lucy gets invited to Thanksgiving dinner!

I believe that experiencing grace is experiencing God, and grace is offered freely and universally. How do we recognize grace? In beauty, nature, love,

compassion, new life. It ignites awe, it inspires artists with color and writers with words. It creates comfort through a sense of overwhelming love, and discomfort in the awareness of the pain of others. It demands a response and offers the hope that if we choose to respond we will be better for it.

The natural world is gift (grace)—undeserved, possibly unintentional, random, unplanned gift. And even if there is no personal God / Divine Parent there is a Source, a First Cause. So whether the Source is a Particle or a Person there is reason to be grateful for that gift. There might have been nothing and yet there is so much more than nothing. There might have been silence but there is music—composed by humans but also built into the very fabric of nature. There might have been only shades of grey and instead there is riotous color.

All of this is miracle, is grace to me.

Grace and Hope

I think I am beginning to see my way through to something meaningful something, dare I say, hopeful. A way of looking at life that allows the possibility that there is more, that there is a much bigger picture, a greater meaning, a deeper value even if it cannot be defined.

Malcolm was an experience of grace in my life. He brought me joy and also the deepest, most excruciating pain and loss. Perhaps that is the price of grace, the pain we suffer in its loss—the loss of love, the loss of inspiration, the loss of a child. It is strange that after the first few years of paralyzing sadness I began to feel as if Malcolm had come back home. I don't feel his absence so much now. It is as if he has taken up lodging inside my heart so I am never alone; I am never without him. Of course I still miss him and sometimes cry involuntarily when I see hair like his or hands like his, or I am reminded of his smile. And sometimes I sob and scream. But it is also possible for me to see the future with hope because he is going forward into the future with me, as part of me. In the end there are no ideas, no philosophies, no theories that can provide me with anything I want more than that.

And what about faith? What about God? Well, for now, I have the idea of grace, and the principle of compassion. I have the love of my husband and son and my extended family. I don't know about the purpose of the universe or the existence of a divine plan. I don't know the purpose of my own existence, either. But I recognize that I have a choice about how to live: hopeful or hopeless. And I choose Hope.

Coming Full Circle

Journal Entry—November 23, 2013

As I write this I am sitting in a theology library at a Dominican Retreat Center, one I used to visit in my role as religion teacher and retreat moderator. It seems so ironic that I have come back here full circle. When I was here last, Katrina was still just a girl's name and Malcolm was still alive; I still practiced my Catholicism in a faith community—my school; I was angry at my church, but it was still my church; I was still sure of God.

And here I am now, trying to finish a book on grief and loss. I didn't originally plan to be writing this weekend, I planned to be reading in preparation for an interview on Monday which hopefully will result in acceptance into a Clinical Pastoral Education program: I have decided my next step is to become a nondenominational Chaplain. My husband is here with some Jesuit boys on retreat, and, as I thought about the experiences that awaited the boys, I found myself nostalgic for those days when I led retreats. It came flooding back to me—the feeling of a palpable energy. It shone through the leaders as they prepared for weeks ahead of time. It was present on retreat when students would open their hearts and tell their stories and pray for help with their burdens.

What was that energy? Was that the God that has been eluding me since Malcolm's death? Or was it just the experience of the power of human compassion and goodness? Then again, is that not a view of God too? The One Power, Supreme Goodness, Universal Life Force that is responsible for the world and with which or with whom the world and everything in it is filled?

Images of God

An Orchestra

While listening to the soaring and sublime music of Eric Whitacre's "Fly to Paradise" I wondered about the image of God as music. I know it's not usual to imagine God in this way but bear with me. Where does the music exist before it is played? It is, if you like, potential music like potential energy in physics. It is represented by symbols on paper but the symbols do not communicate the actual music only the structure of the music. Before it is written it is an idea, an inspiration in a composer's mind. And before that?

Where does music go after it has been played? It has entered into our collective experience. It will never die. And hundreds of attempts will be made to bring it alive again, to remember it, just like rituals and sacraments are used to "re-member," to make newly present, the God of a community's faith or the saving event that first knit them together.

The instruments in the orchestra, each one represents a particular metaphor for God. Single voices with a single theme. Sections represent different religious systems of belief, multi-layered, complex, fitting together but ultimately only a part of the whole.

The music is more than the notes of all the instruments, more than the artistry of an individual musician. Music also involves the intangibles of tone, emphasis, feeling. And every performance creates the music anew.

God, like the music of an orchestra, flows through us—the instruments— but is always greater than anything we can individually or collectively give voice to. When we become channels for God it is fleeting, momentary, and God cannot be contained by us. When our instruments are laid down we experience an emptiness, an absence of God, but when we take up the instrument again and combine our efforts with others we once again experience the soaring rapture of the presence of God moving through us.

A Rope

Author Rabbi Rami Shapiro has an interesting way of talking about God.[4] To explain his perspective he uses the image of a length of rope. Holding the rope

---

[4] *Rabbi Rami's Guide to God: Roadside Assistance for the Spiritual Teacher*, Rabbi Rami Shapiro.

up he makes two knots in it, one represents us and the other someone we love. Each knot is separate and distinct but still joined to the other and each knot is part of the rope and therefore made up of the same essence or "ropeness." Then he unties one knot. The untying represents the death of the one we love. The knot is no longer present as itself. Yet it is in essence still part of the rope and connected to us. If God is the rope then this represents how we are never apart from God and neither are we ever totally apart from those who have died. It is a curiously simple yet profound image.

God as Parent—Revisited

If God is our parent. God is everyone's parent—not just the good guys. Have you ever watched the news and seen a mother doubled over in agony as her son is led off by the police or receives a sentence? That is profound loss. Regardless of the awful things her son may have done (presuming that he is guilty) she loves him. She may hate what he has done but he is still her boy, her lost and wayward child, the smiling face in her family photos.

God is my parent; God is also the parent of my abusers. God suffers as the parent of the one who has been hurt and the parent of the one who has caused that hurt. As an image for God this is suddenly horrific.

Let us consider the story of Jesus. God's son is on the cross, God's other sons put the nails through his wrists and sentenced him to death. God's daughters wept at his son's feet. There's something more here. If God is our parent, not only is God intimately connected to each of us, we are intimately connected to each other. We share blood, we share essence.

When Malcolm died I felt that God had let go. I no longer saw evidence of God or felt God's presence. Had God disappeared? Not completely. God was still there in each of the people around me and Malcolm was still there in each of them too. Not in the separate and distinct way I wanted him to be there but there nonetheless. He was present in the impact he had made on each of the family members and friends who grieved his death. Malcolm is still here in me and in his father and brother in a very special way. In our genes, in our memories, in our hearts. We are still connected; we will always be connected. Knots on the same rope.

Rediscovering Hope

Journal entry—January 4, 2014

This year marks the seventh anniversary of Malcolm's death and it also marks a number of changes in my life. I lost my job in September and that could have been a real crisis. Well, to be honest I thought it was! But in retrospect it turned out to be more blessing than not. I have taken the time to examine where I want to go next, and I have decided it is neither back into Catholic education or into another office job. Instead I am returning to school to pursue training in Chaplaincy. Will it work out? I don't know. But it is exciting to be trying something new.

There is a real sense of freedom when you have nothing to lose and no one to prove anything to. A small inheritance from my parents' provided the fiscal freedom, and the support of my husband provided the emotional freedom.

During this hiatus from work I have refinished lawn furniture and an old desk and chair. I have patch painted a water-stained ceiling, twice—they were very stubborn stains. I have cooked healthy meals and kept a clean house, and enjoyed doing all of this because I knew it was temporary.

The most important change was not home improvement though, it was a change in my outlook. I have rediscovered hope. It wasn't a sudden discovery, it has been creeping up on me slowly and gently for a while now. The reason I didn't pay too much attention was because it was not immediately obvious, the change was not linear but cyclical, just like the grief.

When grief is cyclical you visit the grief over and over again. You face the same questions, the same guilt. Sometimes the grief seems to feel as bad as those first few months, but then you come out of the cycle and your emotions settle down again. The recovery and equilibrium seem to last longer each time and you find that hope lingers just a little more.

Traces of Hope

After coming out of a recent depression I had the opportunity to accompany my husband to a retreat center. The truth was I wasn't ready to be alone for three days and two nights. So, while my husband was working on the high school retreat, I had the weekend to myself while someone else cooked my meals. I brought my writing on grief and loss and thought I might give it a look again. I had been stuck for quite a while on the issue of hope. Since its inception my book had morphed from the theme of grief and loss to the theme of meaning and hope. The trouble was that I wasn't sure what hope I had and what shape it took. For two years I had been thinking and reading and, yes, praying, even though I wasn't sure to whom or for what purpose. Then I sank into depression once more and hope mocked me from the sidelines of my life, yet again. But now I was on the other side of the depression and something had shifted. What I had been reading began to take a meaningful shape. Quotes I had highlighted began to organize themselves, and I found at last I was able to get my head around the possibility of hope. I hoped for hope, and that was closer than I had been in years to actually being hopeful.

So for two full days I wrote. I got to know my book again and began to develop greater coherence. And I worked on the last section, the section that has given the title to the book: *Traces of Hope*. Those were powerful days. I felt invigorated and, dare I say it, hopeful that my book might make sense and prove useful. I wasn't sure how long these feelings would last but it felt really, really good. I even attended some of the retreat sessions and was inspired and awed by the faith of the young men present.

After that weekend I enrolled in the first unit of a program in Clinical Pastoral Care and began training to be a chaplain. I began attending a United Church of Christ with a friend of mine, and I began a practice of daily reflection or meditation, usually at night because I am not worth a damn in the morning. I haven't been consistent but I continue to commit.

Coming Out of the Dark

One evening on the high school retreat with my husband I participated in evening prayer. The prayer began with us all sitting in a circle. Then all the lights were turned off. The retreat center was surrounded by woods so no light

came in from the windows. Being plunged into such absolute darkness was a shock. I couldn't even tell if my eyes were open or closed. The darkness was tangible and airless. Then my eyes adjusted and I began to make out the shapes of furniture and markings on the floor. Then the shapes of people emerged. And next when a candle was lit in the center I realized that even before it was lit, the darkness had not been absolute, light had existed.

The experience of grief and loss is like that experience of absolute darkness in a shuttered hall at night when the lights are suddenly extinguished. The darkness feels like death. But slowly you begin to notice a subtle change. You begin to become aware of your life once again and of people sitting with you in your grief. You felt alone and isolated but you realize you have never been alone. You felt abandoned but come to recognize the support of people who have been there all along. And then joy enters your life again and it is as if a candle has been lit. Nothing is quite as bright as it once was, but you begin to experience that life is worth living.

Slowly the candle's light is passed from one to another and more candles are lit, and light, hope, joy and gratitude spread. The memory of the absolute darkness remains, but the joy and gratitude for the present light dulls the fear and pain of that darkness, and everything you see now is even more precious than it was before. Tears of relief and joy now mix with tears of sadness and fear. Death has been overcome; life goes on. And life is good.

Meaning Rediscovered

I have only completed one unit of Clinical Pastoral Care so far, but chaplaincy work has already had a profound impact. For six months I spent eleven hours a week doing clinical visits in a hospital, and one evening and occasional Saturdays in class. The visits were the best part. I learned what it means to really listen and be present. If the patients didn't want company I would simply offer to pray for them. If they wanted, we would pray together. Sometimes we spent time in life-reflection; sometimes we talked about death. There were often tears. Once I was called upon to help explain to parents the imminent death of their new born; another time I baptized a set of premature twins who subsequently died in their father's arms while we sat together. Often I was asked the same question that prompted this book. Why? And the patient or family member and I would pursue the question together. I have never felt more privileged or more humbled. Privileged to be allowed to walk with someone in their suffering and humbled by the faith of so many who were facing their mortality with grace.

I especially remember a conversation with a Hindu gentleman and his wife. The husband was diagnosed with a form of cancerous growth that the current hospital felt was beyond their expertise to treat. He was being transferred to a specialist cancer center; the prognosis was not good. But he was smiling and hopeful. He was planning a pilgrimage to temples in India once he recovered, and a trip to England to visit old friends. He reflected with me on the state of a world in which people were not kind to each other and did not respect each other or respect life; it made him sad. Sad but not hopeless. He focused on the good he saw around him and trusted in the doctors, even after a close brush with death due to a medical error.

This gentle man and his faith in humanity was a gift of grace to me. In him I saw the compassion and forgiveness extolled by Jesus of Nazareth and Pema Chödrön and by so many of today's spiritual teachers from across religious traditions. When I asked if I might pray for him he answered, *Of course. I would be honored. We all pray to the same God after all.*

I have decided to continue with chaplaincy training and I will enter a full-time residency in the fall. I am learning to listen more and question less. I am learning to be a "healing presence" and create a quiet space within myself where I can set aside personal anxieties and meet with each new person I encounter, offering them my fullest attention. It isn't easy to do that but I am getting better at it. And I'm getting better at praying. I have developed greater comfort with the word God, allowing it to represent the Good to whom all religions pray, the Father to whom Jesus prayed, the Source of life, Grace. Every day I try to spend at least a few minutes in intentional quiet

mindfulness—sitting on the porch, or walking around the neighborhood. Just practicing being present to the moment and quieting the mind.

During my first unit of training in the spring I got into the habit of saying a blessing on my day using words adapted from "Blessing This Day" by author Caroline Myss.[5] In the prayer I commit to focusing only on the day ahead and not on my past or my future, to being grounded in the present moment and being available to each person I meet, to respecting myself and others, and offering compassion and non-judgment. The prayer ends with these words:

> *"And finally, my last prayer is that I commit to trusting in the power of Goodness. With that, I bless my day with gratitude for all that comes."*

I believe in the power of goodness that is innate in all human beings, even those who initially may seem angry and bitter. I recognize that life is both precious and tenuous. And I have developed a greater respect for people's questions.

In the hospital setting, people in crisis, and the ones who love them, have a lot of questions. I am learning how to be present without offering answers, because what is needed at that moment is not speculation, not explanation, but compassion. People want to be heard. They want to feel that they are of value, that their questions are of value, and that they deserve attention. Being in a hospital bed makes people very vulnerable. The defenses of personal clothing and privacy are taken from them. The self-definition they gained from their profession has been at least temporarily withdrawn. They may not have a life-partner or children to sit with them, and questions of meaning and mortality begin to loom large, even for those who are not in immediate danger. What becomes important in those moments is not philosophy or theology but presence, a listening ear, someone to help them recall moments that gave their life meaning, moments when they made a contribution.

---

[5] *God Has No Religion*, Frances Sheridan Goulart.

I sat one day with an older man who had been living on the streets. He had suffered a mild stroke and had been admitted to the hospital. This was his fourth admittance and he was not in good shape. On my first visit he was gruff and uninterested in talking. On my second visit he was eating lunch and I asked if I could sit with him. He said, yes. In between bites we began a conversation about food, a popular New Orleans topic. He eventually admitted that he used to enjoy cooking and had cooked many meals for meetings at an American Legion hall. Then he began talking about a boy scout troop they had sponsored at the American Legion and how he had been a volunteer scout assistant. He didn't have any children of his own, he said, but he remembered trips he went on with the scouts and how he taught the boys to cook over a camp fire. They were tough kids, some without fathers, and a bit hard to handle, but he felt they connected with him. Then he told me how one year their small troop had entered a skills competition and come in third place against much larger troops and how proud he had been of them. One boy later introduced him to his mom as the scout leader, even though he was just the assistant. And that had made him feel so special. As he was telling me this he began crying. I told him how much the boy scouts had helped my two sons grow in confidence, and how the leaders had been like second fathers to them. I suggested that what he had given those boys was much more then camping skills, he had given them life skills. He had made a difference. When he was leaving he asked me to come by again, if I could. I said I would be sure to check in with him.

The previous story illustrates what the search for meaning has come to signify for me. It is about identifying moments of joy and transformation, moments when you have made a difference, and moments when others have recognized your worth. It is about becoming aware of the sacredness and fragility of life, about finding the beauty and grace in each moment. I still enjoy philosophical and theological debates with my husband and son, but I have managed to let go of the need for any ultimate answers. It has become enough, most of the time, to acknowledge the meaning and the giftedness of what is, and not worry about what will be or why.

I pray every day. I pray in thanksgiving for all I that I have and I ask for a blessing on my boys, both of them. I also acknowledge that in the hospital rooms, when I have struggled for the right words in prayer, or when I have sat and held the hand of a dying man for over an hour, I have prayed for help. And help has come. Sometimes from within, from my own strength, or from the words of loved ones I carry with me. Sometimes from the patient who leads me where the prayer needs to go. At other times a doctor or nurse has offered support, or another chaplain has joined me. And I have learned to trust in that help, because I know I am not alone. I am never alone. Unlike the man on his rooftop during the flood, I have learned to recognize when God sends me a boat.

INDEX